GOD AND MAN AS
ONE INSEPARABLE BEING

and

THE POWER OF A DIVINE IDEA

GOD AND MAN AS ONE INSEPARABLE BEING
Address of 1943

and

THE POWER OF A DIVINE IDEA
Address of 1944

MARTHA WILCOX

The Bookmark
Santa Clarita, California

Copyright 2003 by Ann Beals

All rights reserved under the International
and Pan-American Copyright Convention

Library of Congress Control Number: 2003104852

Wilcox, Martha.
   God and man as one inseparable being : association address of 1943 ; The power of a divine idea association address of 1944 / [Martha Wilcox].
   p. cm.
   ISBN 0-930227-53-0

   1. Christian Science. I. Title. II. Title: Power of a divine idea.
BX6945.W63 2003   289.5
                           QB103-200202

Published by
The Bookmark
Post Office Box 801143
Santa Clarita, California 91380

CONTENTS

GOD AND MAN AS ONE INSEPARABLE BEING
Association Address of 1943
page 3

THE POWER OF A DIVINE IDEA
Association Address of 1944
page 49

INTRODUCTION

As the twentieth century physics dissolved the seemingly solid substance of matter into empty space and waves of energy, the effect of thought on the visible form became increasingly obvious. It is now said, "All is consciousness." Everything originates subjectively, and so our lives are our thoughts objectified.

Even before this idea became well known, Martha Wilcox was writing and teaching on the subjective nature of being. As a Christian Science practitioner and teacher, she addressed her students each year on subjects relevant to this Science, especially the power of thought to shape our lives. But she went beyond analyzing the human mind and how it manifests or "out-pictures" itself as our life.

She relates this subjective state of mind to Christian Science and explains how we can so improve or spiritualize our thinking that we can experience healing and regeneration through prayer alone. Few teachers write as lucidly and as deeply on the subjective nature of being as Mrs. Wilcox.

Prayer is a totally subjective experience. If our thoughts are objectified as our life experience, and our prayers affect our thoughts, purifying and spiritualizing them, then the hope of a better life can be found through prayer. And in Christian Science this is exactly what happens. We change how we think as we come to understand God and our relationship to Him. As this spiritual unfoldment takes place subjectively, it objectifies itself in healing and regeneration.

In her address to her students each year, Mrs. Wilcox expands upon the basic ideas found in the Christian Science textbook, *Science and Health with Key to the Scriptures*, by Mary Baker Eddy. Mrs. Wilcox encourages us to study this textbook, examine our thoughts and ask if they are material or spiritual. If all is consciousness, then we can lose our mortal existence only as we come to understand the spiritual nature of reality. These addresses help us to transform consciousness. They enable us to look deep into the reality of all things and pattern our own thoughts after the divine.

   In the 1944 address, Mrs. Wilcox repeated some pages from her 1943 address because her students requested her to do so. Although these pages are a word for word repetition of those in the 1943 address, they have been included in both addresses.

A. B.

GOD AND MAN AS ONE INSEPARABLE BEING
Association Address of 1943

1. The Power of a Right Idea ... 3

2. God and Man as One Inseparable Being ... 14

3. The Importance of Understanding the Divine Idea ... 21

4. Malicious Mental Malpractice ... 27

5. Healing ... 38

GOD AND MAN AS ONE INSEPARABLE BEING
Association Address of 1943

1. THE POWER OF A RIGHT IDEA

One Inseparable Being

In the first section of this morning's lesson, I am presenting for your consideration a spiritual fact that has existed from everlasting to everlasting. This spiritual fact is that *God, or Spirit, and man is one inseparable being*. This spiritual fact always existed in Principle, but it was made visible in concrete form, for the first time, with the birth of Jesus.

This spiritual fact is set forth in our textbook, *Science and Health with Key to the Scriptures*, and reads; "The Holy Ghost, or divine Spirit, (which is the same impersonal divine Science that we are using today) overshadowed the pure sense of the Virgin-mother with the full recognition that being is Spirit." To us, this means that anything that is being, when correctly understood, is Spirit, or God.

This revelation that man is in oneness and sameness with Spirit, or that Spirit, God, and His manifestation, man, is one inseparable being, came to Mary's consciousness, and was the result of Mary's self-conscious communion with the Holy Ghost, or the Science of being which was her Mind.

The patriarchs and prophets discerned this spiritual fact as existing in God, or Spirit, and believed that it would be expressed in some future time and some unknown manner. But Mary was the first to give visible, concrete proof to the world of this spiritual fact that "being is Spirit" in the form of Christ Jesus, the Saviour, or the coincidence of the human and the divine.

Students, when we today recognize and give visible proof of any invisible fact that is revealed to our human consciousness, the results are immeasurable!

The greatest thing that can possibly come to human consciousness has come to us in this present age. This greatest thing is the divine idea of God and what He is in manifestation, as one inseparable being. We, as Christian Scientists, will be ready to progress when we live our lives from the standpoint of this revealed truth, that God and His manifestation is one inseparable being — the I AM THAT I AM.

We speak of God, and we speak of man in God's image and likeness, but at times such statements seem either to detach man from God or to attach man to God. But God named Himself I AM THAT I AM. Therefore, it is necessary in the practice of Christian Science that we gain and maintain the right idea of God and His manifestation, as one inseparable being, or as I AM THAT I AM.

In a measure, we all understand the great power of a right idea when it is put into operation in our human consciousness. Everything of value in the world today is the immediate result of the power of right ideas in human consciousness. Everything that is good in government, in religion, in commerce, in art, and in the sciences, is the direct outcome of the power of right divine ideas that have appeared in human consciousness, and have been wrought out into tangible, concrete expression. In order to have spiritual power, it is necessary to have operative in our so-called human consciousness, the right idea of God and His manifestation — man — as one inseparable being.

H. G. Wells said, "Human history is, in essence, a history of ideas." And all history shows us that all great epochs begin with the birth of new right ideas in human consciousness. A new and right idea is the appearance and development of the power of an unseen Principle, but unseen only to the material senses.

Students, do we appraise our ideas correctly? Basically, we should appraise all our right so-called human ideas as being divine ideas. We should appraise the appearance and development of these ideas as proceeding from the unseen divine Principle. We should understand that all our right human ideas have their source, character, essence, and power in divine Mind, in Almighty God, and never in a so-called personal mind. All that is good and useful and natural to the so-called human mind, is but the imperfect appearance of the good and the useful and the natural that is the one and the only Mind.

In Christian Science, all divine ideas that unfold in our human consciousness constitute our understanding, and are man. If we detach these divine ideas from the divine Mind, and appraise them as formed by our so-called human mind, then these ideas, being separated from their divine source, are devoid of the divine power which demonstrates itself.

As Christian Scientists, we should recognize and acknowledge that any right idea in our consciousness is Almighty God in being. As we do this, we find that any idea in our consciousness, is not an abstract, dormant something that we just think about, but is a living, conscious, irresistible power which demonstrates itself and works the works of God.

Sometimes we hear a Christian Scientist say, "The ideas in my consciousness never seem to express themselves visibly." It is our work to know and realize that whenever a divine idea appears in our consciousness, it is not we, as a so-called person, that originates this idea. This idea is Almighty God Himself, here and now, uttering Himself as this idea. He is this idea as living, conscious power and law in operation, and He presents His results or evidence in tangible, concrete proofs or demonstrations.

God and Man as One Inseparable Being

Isaiah's Vision of the Divine Idea

The prophet Isaiah appraised the appearing of the divine idea of God and His manifestation, man, as one inseparable being. When this idea appeared to Isaiah, he appraised it as "unto us a child is born." And immediately he appraised even the first faint appearing of this divine idea as being in the fullness and completeness of its divine character. He appraised this divine idea as "Wonderful, Counselor, The mighty God, The everlasting Father, The Prince of Peace."

If we, like Isaiah, recognize that even the first faint appearance of a right idea in our consciousness is already full, complete, finished, perfect and permanent, the results would be amazing. How few of the infinite ideas that knock at the door of our consciousness are recognized for what they are, and are given admittance and allowed to unfold in their completeness and perfection and permanence! I fear not many of them; they are usually forgotten almost immediately.

When Isaiah, the great Hebrew prophet, wrote the outstanding statement, "For unto us a child is born," this divine idea was far in advance of its tangible, concrete appearance in human consciousness. When Isaiah wrote this prophecy, he was not referring to a little babe lying in a manger; he was referring to a divine idea that already existed in Principle; he was referring to the eternal fact that God and His manifestation is one inseparable being.

Isaiah visioned so-called human life as evolved from God, divine Principle, not from matter or personality. Isaiah visioned man, the infinite idea of God, as begotten of the one Principle of all being; he saw man as untouched by sin and death; he saw Deity as divine Mind manifested; he saw God as the Son made visible; he saw the coincidence of the human with the divine. This, too, was the vision that was born to Mary's human consciousness by the Holy Ghost, or divine Science — and to which Mary gave concrete visible manifestation.

This divine order of being is still the order as presented to us in divine Science. First, there is the vision or revelation of some divine idea in our human consciousness, and later this is followed by the tangible, concrete, visible manifestation of this divine idea to the world. The vision or revelation always becomes tangible concrete unfoldment. The recognition of a divine idea always gives place to the cognition of the divine Mind as being the idea. Far too often, when a divine idea is revealed or recognized, we stop right there. But the revelation of an idea must become tangible concrete unfoldment; the recognition of an idea must become cognition, else the world will learn little of the divine idea.

Isaiah visioned the joy in heaven and on earth when this mighty idea — God and His manifestation, man, as one inseparable being — would be presented in concrete form to the world, even though to material sense this divine idea appeared as a babe. Millions of babies had been born before this particular baby was born in the little town of Bethlehem, but not one of these millions had been heralded by an angel throng or a star in the East.

The Saviour, Christ Jesus

The angel said unto the shepherds, "Fear not: for, behold, I bring you good tidings of great joy, which shall be to all people. For unto you is born this day in the city of David a Saviour, which is Christ the Lord." The angel did not say that a child is born, but he said a Saviour is born and this Saviour is Christ the Lord, the divine idea, the living, conscious, irresistible truth that makes all men free.

This was a remarkable event. Nothing like it had ever appeared on earth before. The narrative continues: "And suddenly there was with the angel a multitude of the heavenly host praising God [not praising a baby], and saying, Glory to God in the highest, and on earth peace, good will toward men." These angel visitants beheld not the human concept called a babe, but they beheld the concrete visible idea, the Saviour. They beheld the in-coming of a new dispensation — the dispensation of God, the Father, made visible as God, the Son.

At this time Caesar Augustus was governor of the Roman Empire, and his supposed power and law was so great that he did as he pleased with the lives and property of millions of people. Never before had a mortal swayed such power, and never again will a mortal sway such power. Why? Because unto us has been born a divine idea, a Saviour. And when correctly appraised as Almighty God, this divine idea, or Saviour, in our human consciousness is irresistible power and law, which demonstrates itself.

When the hosts of heaven heralded the appearance of this divine idea — this Saviour, Christ the Lord — there was being established on earth a permanent empire clothed with such divine power and law, that the seeming material power and law of Caesar Augustus would fade into its native nothingness.

To the shepherds, Jesus was Immanuel. To them Deity had taken on the form of flesh and blood. But Mary's concept of man had risen above matter and material sense, and while others might see man as flesh and blood, Mary's idea of man was God's idea of Himself — the Christ. Mary's mode of consciousness was Truth — the Christ — and she gave her true conception of man visible birth. Mary fulfilled the prophecy of the prophet Isaiah. Her spiritual conception of the idea man, conceived in her of God, the Holy Ghost, was made visible as God, the Son — Christ Jesus. This was Mary's concrete proof of the supremacy of Spirit, or Mind, over matter, or mortal mind.

By reason of her conception and its visible proof, Mary clearly understood that in every instance, whether it was sin, sickness or death, Christ Jesus was to give to the world the proof of the supremacy of Spirit, or Mind, over matter, or mortal mind. This was Jesus' mission in the world, and this is also our mission, as Christian Scientists, in the world today. We, too, are to give proof of the supremacy of Spirit, or Mind, over matter, or mortal mind. And we do this as we understand that the divine idea is man, the Christ, and not a personality.

Association Address of 1943

Immediate Evidence of the Divine Idea

"There was a marriage in Cana of Galilee and the mother of Jesus was there . . ." (See John 2:1-11). It was at this wedding feast that Mary demanded of Jesus that he give proof or evidence of Spirit, or Mind, over matter, or mortal mind. Mary said to Jesus, "They have no wine." To their sense their supply of wine was exhausted. Indeed, Mary perceived that they had no wine, that is, no inspiration — they had no understanding with which to perceive that the underlying fact of all visible things is inexhaustible. Mary demanded of Jesus that he give proof or evidence of this fundamental, operative, inexhaustible divine Principle, which is our Saviour from all want and lack.

Jesus said to his mother, "Mine hour is not yet come." But this was not Mary's sense of the divine idea. Had she not given the visible proof of the invisible fact of God, as Christ Jesus? Jesus, no doubt, had yet to ascend above the restrictions that material suggestions seemed to impose upon him.

Mary knew that there must be the human evidence or proof of the invisible, inexhaustible God, or infinite good, that underlies all visible things. She knew that the evidence of this fact must be in concrete, tangible, visible form at that very hour. She had the understanding and the absolute faith that God, Mind — the creative cause — is ever in operation, and of necessity must present His own ideas or evidences. Therefore, she could say unhesitatingly to the servants at the wedding feast, "Whatsoever he saith unto you, do it."

Jesus knew that a divine idea or spiritual inexhaustible fact, was underlying the human sense of water; because of this understanding, he turned the human sense of water into wine — that is, he turned the limited sense into an inexhaustible sense, and the human sense of the guests was satisfied. Students, any human sense of need is supplied by the divine idea or the spiritual inexhaustible fact underlying the need, and this idea or fact appears to us in the form that best satisfies our human sense.

At this wedding feast, it was demonstrated for all people throughout the ages that any human sense of need is supplied by the divine idea, or the spiritual, inexhaustible fact underlying the need, and this idea or fact appears to us in the form that best satisfies our human sense of need, whether that sense of need is health, home, money, or business.

Christian Science teaches us that when we look beyond all mortal sense, beyond all limitations, to Mind for the divine fact, we express it instantly. When we look for the fact of Mind, then Mind outlines itself to meet the present need, or in other words, the supply appears spontaneously in the form that best satisfies our highest human sense of that reality.

This coincidence of the divine fact and the human need is our Christ Jesus that is with us always. In Matthew we read, "And, lo, I am with you alway, even unto the end of the world." Not a personal, but an impersonal Saviour is with us unto the end of all sense of need. At the wedding feast, Mind — the Mind of Jesus — spake, and it was done. The water was wine, instead of water. Not an instant intervened between Mind as the inexhaustible fact and the visible evidence of that fact.

Ideas Must Become Tangible

Far too many useful and important ideas appear in our human consciousness and remain there merely as ideas. We fail to present these divine ideas in visible, tangible form. Every right idea that comes to our human consciousness is begotten of God, or Mind, and should be cognized as Almighty God, who of necessity unfolds and presents His own ideas, and evidences them humanly, visibly, and at hand, according to the human sense of need.

Nothing can thwart the power of God or prevent Him from giving to His infinite idea of Himself — man — all good. It is God,

Mind, not we personally, who affirms what He, Himself, is as all right ideas, or right knowing; and nothing can thwart this eternal Mind from bringing to light man's eternal oneness with infinite good.

Mrs. Eddy once said, "To affirm that which is true, is to assert its possibility, — to assert it even in the face of all contrary evidence." Students, when we affirm that something is possible, then it is assured, is certain, is vouched for, and is enforced.

She also said, "By affirming that to be true, but which to all human reasoning or sight seems not to be true at all, you can bring it to pass." The power and infinitude of Mind makes every affirmation of Truth instantly available. When we affirm a fact, we are asserting or enforcing the possibility of that fact. By affirming that which is true, we can bring it to pass, because the bringing of it to pass is simply the recognition in our own consciousness of that which already is.

What a vision of success and achievement is unfolded to us when once we understand that God and man — good and its manifestation — is one inseparable being. What certainty and assurance come to us when we appraise even the first faint idea that appears in our consciousness as a divine, inexhaustible fact, as the Almighty God, and therefore as already full, complete, finished, perfect and permanent. More and more should we demand of ourselves that we give proof or evidence of this fundamental, operative, divine Principle which is our Saviour. And as we put this divine Principle to work in our consciousness, we, too, shall see the coincidence of the human need with the divine fact.

Summary

Students, in this lesson, I have endeavored to set forth the origin, the character, the continuity, and the immeasurable power of a divine idea when it appears in human consciousness. Last year, under the subject, "Idealism and Realism" we learned that we might possess a wealth of wonderful ideas; but unless these ideas were wrought out into tangible visible expression, the world would be but little benefited. We brought out the fact that Christ Jesus was our example of a true idealist, because he had the kingdom of ideas within himself. And he was also our example of a true realist, because he demonstrated his kingdom of ideas to be visible facts at hand.

Today, we have learned how Isaiah, the great Hebrew prophet, visioned the unlimited power of a divine idea, and prophesied concerning the power of this idea many years before it was made visible to the world. He appraised the appearing of this divine idea — "Unto us a child is born" — as "the mighty God" who would present His own ideal, or Saviour, in tangible, visible form to a darkened world. Many persons, when thinking of a Saviour, begin their thinking with the birth of Jesus. But the divine idea or Saviour has existed throughout all eternity. The divine idea — God and man as one being — was Mary's immaculate conception and is our Saviour.

Many persons think of Mary as merely incidental to the birth of Jesus, when in reality the Saviour of all things was incidental to Mary's pure conception of man's real being. Mary's concept of man rose above matter and material sense. Her mode of consciousness was divine Science, and she gave her true conception of man visible birth as Christ Jesus — the Saviour. The greatest epoch of history came in when Mary fulfilled the prophecy of Isaiah. When the Holy Ghost, or divine Science, appeared to Mary's consciousness in the form of the right idea of God and man as one being, this fact was evidenced forth as the Saviour of all mankind.

Up to this time there was in the thought of the people but one dispensation — the dispensation of God, the Father. Now, the motherhood and womanhood of God entered thought also, and with the birth of Christ Jesus there appeared a new dispensation — the dispensation of God, the Son. It was through the pure consciousness of Mary that the Trinity of the Godhead was made visible: God, the Father, God, the Son, and God, the Holy Ghost.

These are being expressed in their fullness today in the human and divine coincidence.

Mary gave to the world a Saviour, an impersonal Saviour. She gave to the world the ever-unfolding proof or evidence of the supremacy of Spirit, or Mind, over matter, or mortal mind. But because the world might not understand Mary's demonstration of Mind over matter, she had Jesus demonstrate it again in a simpler form at the wedding feast. At this wedding feast, it was proved that the underlying fact of all visible things is inexhaustible; and as we accept and make active this fact in our consciousness, it becomes our Saviour from every want or need.

Mary knew (and she knew that Jesus knew) that God, divine Mind, is ever-conscious good, and of necessity presents His own ideas in visible evidence. At the wedding feast the spiritual, inexhaustible fact underlying the need of wine appeared to the guests in the form that satisfied their need. Jesus gave the proof that when we look beyond all mortal sense, beyond all limitations to the facts of Mind, we express these facts instantly. At this wedding feast the proof was given for all ages that not an instant intervenes between the inexhaustible facts of Mind and the visible evidence of these facts.

The star of the east symbolizes divine Science. It was the star of divine Science that guided the wise men to the birth of a more spiritual idea — even the Virgin-mother's immaculate conception and visible presentation of man's real being. It is so necessary that we let divine Science guide our thought to this true idea of God and man as one being, and that we accept and demonstrate this true idea in our daily lives. This true idea of God and man as one being, will prove to be our Saviour from all personal sense — from all want, and all age, and all sin, disease, and death.

Students, in *Miscellaneous Writings*, Mrs. Eddy puts the following question to us individually. She asks, "Are we duly aware of our own great opportunities and responsibilities? Are we prepared to meet and improve them, to act up to the acme of divine energy wherewith we are armored?"

2. GOD AND MAN AS ONE INSEPARABLE BEING

Knowing God Aright

Since our individual concept of God and our individual concept of ourself governs our daily life and all its activities, it is necessary to appraise both God and ourself correctly. We should understand that God, the infinite unity of all good, continues Himself out into His manifestation of all good, or man. We should understand that there is not both God and man as separate entities, but there is just God manifested as one being. If the question were put to each of us this morning, "To what extent and how definitely correct is your concept of man?" we would find that we must lift up ourselves and all that constitutes us humanly, as the serpent was lifted up in the wilderness. We must lift up ourselves and all that constitutes us humanly to the level of God — to the level of Truth.

It is necessary to know God aright before we can know ourselves aright, or know anything in the universe aright. We know God aright when we understand Him as one being — being all things or all ideas in indissoluble unity, as one whole, or all. We are willing to appraise God as one being, but we often fail to appraise Him as being all — that is, *as being all men and all things as one indivisible unity or entity.*

Christian Science teaches us to think of God, not as a person in the human sense, but as an all-inclusive totality, as "the sum total of the universe" — the sum total of all existing things. Christian Science teaches that God is the one and only entity or existence; that God is the one and only self or infinite person; that He exists naturally and eternally; that He is self-existent and continuous; that He has no beginning and no ending. In *Miscellaneous Writings*, Mrs. Eddy says, "God is a divine Whole, and All, an all-pervading intelligence and Love, a divine, infinite Principle." When we think of God in this manner, we know that sin, disease, and death are impossible.

I AM THAT I AM

To understand God aright and to practice from this right standpoint, is immeasurably important to the Christian Science student. God, Mind, the I AM, is consciously and constantly affirming of Himself I AM ALL, I AM THAT I AM. To Himself God, or I AM, is consciously and constantly a Whole and All. This understanding of God, or I AM, forever excludes the mistaken concept of a material, corporeal, personal I am. All there is to the so-called personal I am, is merely our false limited concept of the one and only I AM, or God. The so-called personal I am is merely a mistaken concept that we have of ourselves.

Unless we are mentally alert, we think constantly of ourselves as a personal I and of what this personal I is. But the only I AM is God, or Mind, and THAT I AM is His manifestation, or man, as one inseparable being. We do not think of I AM, or God, as out there or over there, separate and apart from ourselves; but rather do we think of I AM THAT I AM as inseparable and pervading this very place, right here where the so-called personal I seems to be. We think of God, or I AM, as filling this very place; we think of Him as divine Mind, eternal Life, the substance and very being, or existence, of all that is in manifestation here as our spiritual selfhood.

We like to think of God, I AM, or divine Principle, as alive, as conscious, as intelligent being — right here and everywhere as our spiritual mental self. We like to think of God, I AM, or divine Principle, as governing and controlling with infinite intelligence and great wisdom every existing thing in His compound of ideas; governing and controlling aright every action, every faculty, every motive, purpose, circumstance and event to the slightest detail.

All students of divine Science like to think of God, I AM, the Mind or divine Principle of all things, as consciously imbued with Love; as yearning to bless and enrich His universe and manifestation — man — with beauty, grandeur and immortality. We should always think of our divine Principle, conscious Life, or Mind, as being the cause, substance, consciousness, intelligence, life, vitality, and sustaining power of every individual, and of every existing thing in the universe.

Everything that we know humanly — that is, everything that is good and useful and natural to our human existence — when correctly understood, is right now a spiritually mental idea and never a material thing. And we, as students of divine Science, should understand and appraise all so-called things of which we are conscious as the immediate phenomena of God, and as spiritually mental, but never as material.

Students, let me repeat: *We should understand and appraise everything — that is, every idea of which we are conscious — as the immediate exhibit or the immediate presence of our divine Mind, or our divine Principle. We should appraise the thing, or idea, which we see and know humanly, as God, or I AM, being that thing, or idea, right here and now.*

In our textbook Mrs. Eddy writes, "By its own volition, not a blade of grass springs up, not a spray buds within the vale, not a leaf unfolds its fair outlines, not a flower starts from its cloistered cell." And in "Voices of Spring" she writes: "In sacred solitude divine Science evolved nature as thought, and thought as things. This supreme potential Principle reigns in the realm of the real, and is 'God with us,' the I AM. As mortals awake from their dream of material sensation . . . infinite Mind is seen kindling the stars, rolling the worlds, reflecting all space and Life, — but not life in matter." (*Miscellaneous Writings*)

Students, we should lift up every human concept to the level of the divine idea. We should translate and understand every human concept as being the immediate presence of God. We should understand that our universe of ideas is forever revealing and declaring I AM as THAT I AM. When we understand and appraise every idea that appears in our consciousness as the immediate object of divine Mind, we shall have no difficulty in proving the indestructibility, the immortality, the immutability, the omnipresence of that idea, or so-called thing.

How many of us appraise a tooth, a heart, or a lung, as the immediate phenomenon of Mind, and not as a material object of sense? A tooth, a heart, a lung, all things, or ideas, all thought-forms, are indwelling in the I AM, and are in oneness and sameness with I AM, just as each ray of the sun is indwelling in the sun and is in oneness and sameness with the sun. All infinite ideas, or so-called things, all faculties, all qualities and attributes, are what I AM, God, our own Mind, consciously is to Himself and as Himself.

All infinite ideas, or all existing things, are the essence or the subjectiveness of what God is as Himself. Each idea, each faculty, each quality and attribute is the mighty God, Himself, right here in being. In short, whatever makes up cognitive consciousness is the essence or subjectiveness that constitutes I AM, or God, and this same essence and subjectiveness likewise constitutes His manifestation — man.

In our textbook Mrs. Eddy emphasizes the fact that qualities and attributes give substance and existence to I AM, God, and make I AM, God, what He is in His substance and character. This is true, just as the qualities or elements of oxygen and hydrogen give substance and existence to water, and make water what it is in its character.

Man is the Qualities and Attributes of God

Let us now consider some of the qualities and attributes that constitute I AM, or God, and that likewise constitute the conscious manifestation of these qualities and attributes as man. We should always think of I AM in His universal qualities, as being omnipotent, omniscient, and omnipresent; and we should think of His idea of Himself — man — as being these same universal qualities continued out into conscious manifestation as omnipotence, omniscience, and omnipresence, as oneness and sameness with the omnipotent, omniscient, and omnipresent God — for God and man are one in being.

Let us think of I AM, God, as being the quality or attribute of supremacy, sovereignty, capacity, ability, power. Let us think of Him as being the great 'able-to-do-all-things.' And let us think of all these qualities as being continued out into manifestation, or man.

Let us think of God, or I AM, in His quality of freedom — without restriction or limitation or being circumscribed — and let us think of this quality of freedom as continued out into manifestation, or man. Let us think of I AM — our own Mind — in its qualities of clarity, explicitness, and legibility without confusion, doubt or uncertainty. Let us think of His sanity, vitality, veracity, vivacity and spontaneity, and then think of each individual man, woman and child as the conscious being of these qualities.

Let us think of the qualities of omni-action, infinity, universality, incorporeality, and of man as the conscious identity of these same qualities. Think of the qualities of indestructibility, immutability, immortality, eternality, and know that every idea in the compound of ideas, man, is being these same qualities in substance and character and is "alive for evermore."

We should think of God, I AM, as being the qualities of goodness, kindness and gentleness; of poise, quietness and serenity. And, since these qualities are the essence and subjectiveness of I AM, or God, they are also the essence and subjectiveness of His manifestation — man.

We should think of God, I AM, in His qualities or characteristics of form and color, of infinite variety, of beauty, grandeur, comeliness, grace, charm, freshness and fairness. Man, or manifestation, is the conscious identity of all these qualities or characteristics, and is in oneness and sameness with them. We should think of God, I AM, as being the qualities of happiness, home, companionship, leisure, joy, harmony, love. Man as manifestation is constantly, consciously being in oneness and sameness with these qualities.

We like to think of God, I AM, as being in His substance and character, the qualities of adequacy, abundance, affluence, completeness, perfection, satisfaction, contentment. Man, or manifestation, is the showing forth of this same substance and character. We like to think of God, I AM, as being the living, conscious, irresistible qualities of wholeness, strength, health, energy, and unfailing vigor, and we like to think of ourselves as in conscious oneness with these qualities.

We think of God, I AM, in His qualities of purity, sincerity, patience, truthfulness, righteousness and divinity, and we should think of ourselves as the conscious identity of these same qualities. Think of His qualities of adhesion, cohesion, attraction; His qualities of perception, discernment, apprehension, comprehension, activity, zeal, unfoldment, progress, perpetuity, continuity, constancy, permanency, and obedience. And, students, how we do need to show forth God's quality of permanency, because when once we understand and prove the quality of permanency, we shall manifest eternal Life in all things. It is also important to emphasize God's quality of obedience. He is ever obedient to His own will, and we are obedient to one and the same will.

We like to think that we are in oneness and sameness with the qualities of His holiness, might, wisdom, mercy, justice, and judgments. We like to think of I AM, God, as ever being the quality of consciousness, as ever being alive, as ever being intelligent, and as all-intelligence, as all-understanding, as all-knowing, all-acting, all-seeing, all-feeling, all-speaking, all-hearing, all-being, all-thinking, all-talking; and we like to think of all these qualities as being continued out into visible manifestation, as man. We might go on *ad infinitum* in naming the qualities of God that are His visible manifestation as man.

Man reveals God, I AM, in all these qualities and attributes. Man, divinely endowed, shows forth all these qualities and attributes. Man is the conscious identity or visible evidence of all the qualities or ideas that God is being. These qualities or attributes are not peculiar to just one person, or to just a few persons, but are expressed by all mankind. And these qualities or attributes are manifested humanly in the proportion that we recognize them as the essence and subjectiveness of the spiritual selfhood of everyone. In the measure that such qualities and attributes are seen as emanations of the divine Mind, they belong to all alike.

Students, we as the son of man — the human manifestation of the Son of God — must be lifted up to the level of God, or Truth. And all that constitutes us humanly, must be lifted up to the level of God, or Truth. We should never think of a great God, a universal I AM, and then think of man as finite, personal, material or mortal. God, I AM THAT I AM, infinite Mind, is indeed great beyond all conception; but so is man — His manifestation — great beyond all conception. How could man as effect, be otherwise than as great as God is great? Man is an infinite effect of an infinite cause, and cause and effect is one being. Man exists for the sole purpose of glorifying God, and he is the full representation of God, in-dwelling in his divine Principle and in oneness and sameness with his divine Principle.

We read from our textbook, "Knowing that Soul and its attributes were forever manifested through man, the Master healed the sick, gave sight to the blind, hearing to the deaf, feet to the lame, thus bringing to light the scientific action of the divine Mind on human minds and bodies and giving a better understanding of Soul and salvation."

3. THE IMPORTANCE OF UNDERSTANDING THE DIVINE IDEA

What I say in this paper may seem to be a reiteration of what has been said in the two previous papers, but I repeat for a purpose. It is imperative that we understand the importance of the divine idea. The divine idea should be so definitely registered in our thought, that we naturally and spontaneously translate so-called material things back into divine ideas.

Things are Really Divine Ideas

What we call material things, when correctly understood, are divine ideas. *The thing and the divine idea are not two, but one.* There is not a thing and a divine idea — *there is divine idea only.* A divine idea is imperfectly seen and known to us as a thing. Whenever we see a thing, it is the human mind seeing its own human concept of some divine idea.

To our human sense, so-called things appear to be structural; that is, they seem to have weight and density, finiteness and boundary, but we know that God's, or Mind's, creation consists entirely of infinite divine ideas that are not structural. Things seem to be structural to us, because our thought is not sufficiently spiritualized to see thoughts, or divine ideas, without material accompaniments.

If we correctly understood the fact that all so-called things are thoughts, or divine ideas, we would have the thing that we desire present, as readily as we have present the thought or human concept about the things. The divine idea is all there is to the so-called thing. When correctly understood, so-called things are distinct and eternal ideas of divine Mind, our Mind, even though they may be imperfectly valued by us. It is because we believe there are both material things and divine ideas, that we have so much difficulty in demonstrating our daily supplies.

We need to understand that the thing is always present, because it is a thought, or divine idea, no matter how it appears to us. The round earth is present as a divine idea, no matter how flat or material or structural it may appear to us. Because a thing is a divine idea, and is "embraced in the infinite Mind and forever reflected," we know that it is always present and always perfect.

The thing, since it is a divine idea, cannot be absent, nor fail, nor be impaired or destroyed, it is only to be appraised correctly. Things, being thought-forms, or divine ideas, are emanations of the divine Mind, our Mind, and always appear to us in forms that we can apprehend in our present state of growth.

The Fundamental Lie

After the divine Mind had finished His creation of divine ideas and pronounced them "good" and "very good," there seemingly took place a very bad dream, wherein there was formed the belief, or lie, that somehow and somewhere, divine ideas became material things. Now, this belief that divine ideas have become material things, is the fundamental lie. Whatever any so-called material thing may seem to do or to be, it is always a lie about the eternal divine idea that is eternally at hand identifying God, or Mind.

It is also necessary that we extinguish the lie of false belief that any thing that constitutes the so-called material body is, in fact, a divine idea. We should never appraise our so-called human body as material. It is, right now, spiritual and divinely perfect. Mrs. Eddy speaks of the human body in our textbook. She says, "The divine Mind, which forms the bud and blossom, will care for the human body, even as it clothes the lily; but let no mortal interfere with God's government by thrusting in the laws of erring, human concepts."

The climax of this lie of false belief, that divine ideas have become material things, is that we have life and consciousness only as we have them through the medium of these material things.

What a travesty! What a misrepresentation! How ridiculous to believe that the heart and liver and lungs and stomach are material things, and that they have the power to regulate and govern our life and our state of consciousness. When shall we learn that the divine Life or consciousness is the substance, the essence, the life and intelligence of every divine idea that constitutes the so-called human body?

Everything in the universe pertaining to the human concept, whether we call the concept an eye, or an ear, or liver, or a tooth, exists as divine idea and has the faculty and the substance of divine Mind. Each divine idea is "embraced in the infinite Mind and forever reflected." All divine ideas are forever present, since they are His omnipresence. They are as eternal as God, or Mind, is eternal. We always have a perfect eye and liver and stomach and teeth, as divine idea; and we have the only one there is, the one that infinite Mind is consciously being.

Appraise All Things Spiritually

Mind's ideas are imperishable. Matter is merely the false sense of a divine idea — a perishable sense of that which is imperishable. But whatever sense we entertain about a divine idea, the fact is that spiritual sense is always present and is the only sense present. This spiritual sense that is always present because it is God's omnipresence, will become more and more apparent to our consciousness as we exercise our reason, practice our revelation, and gain a better understanding of the fact that God is the All and Only and is self-existent.

All ideas, when correctly understood, are divine ideas. Divine Principle must have its divine idea, and this divine idea is co-existent with its Principle. The divine Principle being infinite, its divine idea, likewise, must be an infinite idea. Every idea — bird, tree, flower, hand, heart, tooth, and one's way of making a living — is eternally revealing and declaring and reflecting its divine Principle, Mind. All ideas make up the subjectiveness, or the conscious essence, of God, or Mind. Each and every idea in the whole universe, being the conscious substance and essence of divine Principle, or Mind, is established forever in Principle, or Mind, and is eternal and indestructible in its nature.

Since all causation is Spirit, or Mind, then the universe of ideas must be spiritual. Everything that we are humanly conscious of in a natural way exists in a spiritual and divine way. The bird, tree, flower, landscape, rock, house, hand, eye, arm, foot, tooth, and one's way of making a living — all are divine ideas and all are spiritual. They do not exist as matter, as they appear to material sense; but they exist as spiritual, divine ideas.

The term *idea* is not just another name for a thing. Every so-called thing that is good and useful and natural is a divine idea, and not a material thing at all. When we appraise so-called things correctly, and understand them as they are in fact, we prove them to be divine ideas, instead of the material things they appear to be.

A divine idea never began. It has always existed as an eternal fact, the eternal fact of God, or Mind, in particular manifestation. Divine ideas are always divine, no matter if the material senses do make them appear as material things. It means much in treatment when we know that every divine idea indwells in its cause, as effect; that every divine idea is God, Himself, consciously present. It means much in treatment when we know that each divine idea in the universe of ideas indwells in oneness and sameness with God, or Mind, as the immanence, the subjectiveness, and conscious essence of God, or Mind.

The Human and Divine Coincidence

Let us cease thinking of ourselves as just the mere reflection or showing forth of God. We are more than a reflection. We are what God is; we are God's being; we are God's omnipresence, His omnipotence, His omniscience; we are His divine idea of Himself. The infinite wisdom, intelligence, Truth, and Life that is God, is the same infinite wisdom, intelligence, truth and life that is the substance and conscious essence of His manifestation — man.

The divine idea must be expressed humanly. We must demonstrate the divine fact of man in human consciousness. Man — the compound of all divine ideas — must be in evidence as our human good. This demonstration in our human consciousness, is our Christ that is with us always. Christ is never a person. Christ is a divine coincidence, wherein all divine ideas are reduced to human perception and understanding. (See *Science and Health* 561:16.)

Students, without false humility, we should claim these purely divine ideas that come so clearly to our consciousness, and we should claim them as divine ideas and not as material things. The appearance of these divine ideas in our thought, is the divine Mind interpreting itself to us; and if these ideas are made active as our consciousness, they will lift us out of all depression, limitation, sin, sorrow, war and death, and establish us on a level with God, as effect. These divine ideas have their being in divine Principle, and are the divine Principle in perfect expression and in perfect operation.

Man does not evolve ideas. To human sense it may seem that he does, but we know that divine Mind evolves all ideas and their corresponding identities. Then what do we think when we say the word *man*? When we say *man*, we do not think of a personality with creative power in and of himself. When we say *man*, we think of all the infinite divine ideas that comprise the compound of ideas that manifests God, or Mind. These divine ideas constitute each one of us as individual man. And in the measure that we claim and accept these ideas, and let them be operative as our human consciousness, we enlarge our spiritual universe.

Students, are we aware of the fact that we build our universe in our own individual consciousness? The spiritual universe that is ever present for us to accept, is to us either a spiritual or a material universe, according to the sense we entertain about it. We either build our universe according to the fact that all things are divine ideas, one with divine Mind and hence spiritual and perfect, or else we build it according to our false belief that all things are material, with power in and of themselves. There is but one universe, the universe of divine ideas. Our work as Christian Scientists is to lift the first faint appearance of a divine idea in our consciousness to the level of God, or Mind.

William Thackeray, the great master of English literature, has so wonderfully expressed our universe within. He says: "We view the world with our own eyes, each of us, and we make from within us the world which we see."

4. MALICIOUS MENTAL MALPRACTICE

The term malicious mental malpractice is not a pleasing term, but the name given to any claim, whether pleasing or otherwise, is of little moment. In her writings, Mrs. Eddy has analyzed this term *malicious mental malpractice* and all that it implies, clearly and completely, and she stresses the importance of understanding what it is and what it is not.

What is malicious mental malpractice? In its final analysis, *malicious mental malpractice is revealed as the sum total of iniquity — the complete negation of the divine Mind.* The word *malicious* means "with deadly intent;" the word *mental* means "within the realm of mind;" the word *malpractice* means "wrong practice." Hence, the complete meaning of the term *malicious mental malpractice* is "wrong or evil practice with destructive intent, in the realm of our own thought."

At the present time, we are keenly awake to the suggestions that malicious practices are going on within the realm of the human mind. Each gun, shell, bomb, and tank is the visible expression of some malicious purpose to kill or destroy. And just to say that this seeming evil is nothing and is not going on at all, fails to make good sense, unless we in some degree give proof of such statements.

The time has arrived when every Christian Science student must give proof that evil minds and evil purposes are nothing and are not going on. We, as Christian Scientists, do not associate evil minds or evil purposes with God — the one and only Mind — any more than we associate the mistakes or false statements in our mathematical problems with the principle of mathematics.

The principle of mathematics is a law of annihilation to everything contrary to this principle — not because the principle of mathematics knows anything contrary to itself, but because it excludes the false statements about mathematics whenever it is made active as our consciousness. In like manner, God — the divine Principle of man and the universe — is an ever-operative Principle, and when made active as our consciousness, it annihilates or excludes every misstatement or misconception about God and man. A consciousness of infinite good excludes the possibility of anything contrary to or unlike good.

In *The Christian Science Journal* of August 1890, Mrs. Eddy wrote as follows: "It is my impression that at least a half century will pass away before man is permitted to render his public verdict on some of the momentous questions that are now agitating the world. Also, the discussion of malicious animal magnetism had better be dropped until Scientists understand clearly how to handle this error, — until they are not in danger of dwarfing their growth in love, by falling into this lamentable practice in their attempts to meet it. Only patient, unceasing love for all mankind, — love that cannot mistake Love's aid, — can determine this question on the Principle of Christian Science."

Throughout her writings Mrs. Eddy stresses the fact that Christian Scientists must grow to the understanding of the oneness and allness of the divine Principle, God, and let this understanding dispel from their thought all insistent and persistent suggestions that there are many evil minds and many evil purposes.

A half century and more has passed, and still this subject of malicious mental malpractice — of how evil seems to be and yet is not — needs to be much more clearly understood. Surely in this day Christian Scientists ought to present this subject with more universal wisdom and clarity of understanding than it has been presented in the past.

Many students of Christian Science still believe that there are many evil minds that can, in and of themselves, exercise the power to harm and destroy; many students fear these seeming evil minds; and according to the hearing of the ear, there is much malicious mental malpractice going on among Christian Scientists themselves. Many Christian Scientists are trying to defend themselves from what they believe is directed malicious mental malpractice from others when mental malpractice is wholly within the realm of their own mentality.

There is no other one thing, in the metaphysical practice of Christian Science, that is so misunderstood and so misused as is this term *malicious mental malpractice*. But now, after fifty years of growth, it is being understood wholly as impersonal evil, and is not associated with a person or persons at all. Malicious mental malpractice is now proved to be a negative or ignorant mental state within our own realm of thought. It is wholly a supposititious opposite of infinite Mind or divine Principle. It is now proved not to be mind at all, and we handle it as the negation or denial of the one divine Mind, or as the negation or denial of the truth that is in our own individual thought.

As we understand that malicious mental malpractice, which seems so formidable, is purely negation or ignorance of Truth, and that we contact it only within the realm of our own thinking — never from a person or from without — and as we understand that the active divine Principle that constitutes our own mind will annihilate this supposititious opposite at the point of our own belief in it, then we shall cease to fear it. This divine Principle that is our understanding, is omnipresent, omniscient and irresistible in power, and will annihilate every negation and every state of ignorance that seems to be our mind. As we recognize this fact, evil is as powerless before it as darkness is before the light.

Understanding Eliminates Malicious Mental Malpractice

Because of the prevalent mistaken sense among Christian Scientists about malicious mental malpractice, let us review some of the points already spoken of.

FIRST: What is the character of malicious mental malpractice? Malicious mental malpractice is a mental negation that denies the positive statement of Truth; it is a state of ignorance about God and man as one being; it is the supposititious opposite of infinite Truth, or infinite good; it is the persistent and insistent suggestion that there is an absence of spiritual understanding, or an ignorance of infinite good. Malicious mental malpractice is absolutely nothing when unattached from our belief in it, just as the flatness of the earth is nothing when unattached from our belief in it.

SECOND: Why does malicious mental malpractice appear, today, in the myriad forms of evil, such as sin, sickness, death, war, limitation, confusion, poor business conditions, and so on? Why do we have such a flood of evil beliefs? This is because there is appearing on the horizon of thought an infinitude of good. The supposititious opposite of this infinite good appears to us as infinite evil. But this seeming evil — this mental malpractice operating as our consciousness — is merely the false belief or ignorant sense that we entertain about the fact of infinite good that is appearing.

THIRD: Where does malicious mental malpractice seem to operate? It always operates within the realm of our own thinking, and always as a conflict between seeming evil and the fact of infinite good. And, students, it is so necessary that we have an understanding of divine Principle great enough to annihilate the suggestion that there is a seeming evil that can contend against infinite good.

We are admonished by the wise man to "get understanding." In *Science and Health*, Mrs. Eddy tells us, "the nothingness of nothing is plain; but we need to understand that error is nothing." We all know that ignorance of mathematics is nothing, but it is only as we understand the principle of mathematics that we can prove that ignorance is nothing. With the understanding of the principle of any subject, ignorance on that subject will disappear.

The question is sometimes asked, Does malicious mental malpractice ever serve a divine purpose? Christian Science answers: Yes, the denial or the reverse of Truth or good, which is malicious mental malpractice, does serve a divine purpose. Our textbook says, "If you wish to know the spiritual fact, you can discover it by reversing the material fable." Jesus said, "I am not come to destroy, but to fulfill." Jesus never destroyed the material fable, but by reversing the so-called material fable, he revealed the spiritual fact.

Any evil, or negation of Truth, needs only to be reversed; we never need to destroy it or fear it. A right understanding of what we believe to be a malicious, evil personal mind, eliminates all hatred and fear of persons, places and things from our thought, and we see Truth as the only presence. To the student of understanding, malicious mental malpractice is not an intelligent devil going around like a roaring lion seeking whom he may devour. The student of understanding knows that malicious mental malpractice is only the supposititious opposite of Truth, or infinite good, and that its seeming function is wholly within his own mentality.

How often the active divine Principle within us — that "true Light, which lighteth every man that cometh into the world" — says to you and to me, You are an immortal, spiritual, individual being now. And immediately the seeming opposite of the truth, which is mental malpractice, says, No, that statement is abstract and remote, you are now a mortal, material, personal man, and so is every other individual. What, students, are we to do to answer this claim?

We can get more understanding, that is what we can do! As we gain more understanding of the science of mathematics, we find that the ignorant sense that we entertained ceases to resist our understanding of mathematics. Likewise, as we gain more understanding of divine Science, we find that the ignorant sense of evil, called mental malpractice, ceases to resist our understanding of divine Science. With an increased understanding of divine Science, we cease to fear malicious mental malpractice or even believe that it is going on.

There is no opposition to what we do not yet understand of Truth. Other Christian denominations that are not awake to divine Science, or Truth, are not troubled with the belief of malicious mental malpractice. This makes it clear that it is our understanding, or the truth that is our thinking, that we are to protect and defend.

Malicious mental malpractice does not operate 'over there' outside our own mentality. It always operates within our own mentality as a denial of the truth that we know. As Christian Scientists, our work is to protect and defend this Christ-child, this truth or understanding of divine Science that is our consciousness.

"Defense Against Malpractice"

There are many Readers in Christian Science churches in this audience, and to hold such a position you have attained a degree of the understanding of divine Science. To many who hold such positions, the insistent mesmeric suggestions come that you have reached a standstill; that your reading is not improving; that the congregation is saying that you are not reading as well as you did; that you make mistakes, and so on.

Now, your work as a Reader in a Christian Science church is to protect and defend the truth that is your present mentality from mesmeric suggestions. This protective work that you do will not only protect and defend the truth in your own mentality, but will protect and defend the truth of every mentality in your congregation, because each and every mentality is the one and the same infinite Truth.

Mrs. Eddy gives us a very simple rule in our *Manual* under the heading "Defense against Malpractice." She tells us "never to return evil for evil, but to know the truth that makes free." By this she means that when the suggestion comes to our consciousness that some person is thinking evilly about us, then we should not return evil for evil by thinking and believing that there is a personality who can think evil or one who can return evil thoughts. Such thinking would be mental malpractice in us. When we know the truth that makes free, there is no personality either to think evil thoughts or to receive evil thoughts, since God is the only thinking agent.

Association Address of 1943

In *Miscellaneous Writings*, under the subject "Taking Offence," Mrs. Eddy writes, "The mental arrow shot from another's bow is practically harmless, unless our own thought barbs it. It is our pride that makes another's criticism rankle, our self-will that makes another's deed offensive, our egotism that feels hurt by another's self-assertion. Well may we feel wounded by our own faults; but we can hardly afford to be miserable for the faults of others."

From our textbook, we learn that divine Mind is the only enactor, the only thinking agent; and Mind sees and knows His own infinitude, and sees and knows it as good, complete and perfect. This infinite Mind says, "I am All. A knowledge of aught beside Myself is impossible." (*Unity of Good*) With such facts of divine Principle established as our thought, are we to sit supinely by and fail to protect and defend this Principle of divine Science, which is our thought, from mesmeric suggestions?

The sole intent and purpose of mental malpractice — these insistent arguments that seem to take place within our mentality — is to silence and destroy the truth or understanding that we have gained of God, divine Principle. Our work, as a Christian Scientist, is to let this active divine Principle which is our understanding, meet and annihilate these insistent suggestions at the point of our own belief in them.

God is All and Evil is Nothing

We should handle — that is, make nothing of — these malicious suggestions within the realm of our own thought, and handle them as negation, nothing. Too many of us affirm the truth in a remarkable degree, but vigorously resist the evil as something, and utterly fail to let the divine Principle which is our understanding dispel or annihilate these false mesmeric suggestions and thereby set ourselves free.

Mrs. Eddy wrote our textbook in order to establish just one thing to the world, and this one thing is: "All is infinite Mind and its infinite manifestation, for God is All-in-all." And while Mrs. Eddy said that God is infinite, All, she also established the fact that "there is no evil." These are two statements of one fact. These two statements have brought about an acknowledgment that, irrespective of appearances, divine Mind is the substance and being of all visible things in our universe, and that these so-called visible things are nothing but infinite Mind and its infinite manifestation. Therefore, to infinite Mind, or infinite good, there is no evil.

This acknowledgment will soon be followed by the further enlightenment that since Mind is infinite All, and good, then what appears to be matter in our universe, when correctly understood, is Mind, or Spirit; and what appears to be evil in our universe, when correctly understood, is good and very good.

Students, when shall we cease calling our universe of Spirit, matter? When shall we cease calling our universe of good, evil? We build our universe according to our individual understanding and acceptance of infinite good, or we build it according to our belief in evil.

Our textbook says, "Material sense defines all things materially." But with understanding, or spiritual sense, we learn that we do not need to change things and conditions in our universe; but we do need to change our false material sense of our universe into a spiritual sense of our universe. We need to change our false belief about our universe into a state of understanding, and this is done wholly within the realm of our own mentality.

In Genesis it is recorded that all creation is good and very good. In Revelation, we find the full uncovering of evil as nothing, set forth in a metaphysical statement of fact. This uncovering of all evil as nothing was dictated to St. John by Christ Jesus, who commanded him to write it in a book and send it to the seven churches of Asia. This full uncovering of the deceptive mental character of all evil as nothing, was recorded by St. John in symbols; and when these symbols are translated into ordinary speech, they are very helpful and enlightening.

Association Address of 1943

The Beast, the False Prophet and the Dragon

According to St. John's allegory, there were two great forces of evil that claimed to rule the world and claimed to destroy those who failed to worship them. The first force of evil, a physical force, was called 'the beast.' The second force of evil, a mental force, was called 'the false prophet.' These two forces stood for materiality and false mentality. But according to the allegory — and this is the point that needs to register in our thought — neither beast nor false prophet, that is, neither materiality, nor false mentality, had the slightest power of their own because they were phenomena, or effect, only. They were said to have "power . . . and great authority" only because it was given to them by the third figure in the allegory — the great red dragon.

What is the dragon? St. John defines the dragon as "the Devil and Satan, which deceiveth the whole world." And, today, this same dragon is deceiving us much of the time. The great red dragon — Devil or Satan — is never a person, power, nor presence that attacks and harms us; but it is a mental state of deception which insists that the opposite of Truth is true; which insists that sin, war, disease, age and death are the effects of divine Mind — the one and only cause.

The dragon is not a person nor an evil force, but is the insistent mental suggestions or mesmeric arguments that seem to enter the thought of the Christian Scientist, and persistently insist that the truth which he affirms is not true now, but that the opposite of the truth is true now. The dragon says to you and to me, "God is not all. You have a separate mind from God, a mind of your own, and I can manipulate your mind and make you believe in what does not and could not exist from the standpoint of Truth." The dragon, — so-called mortal mind, personal sense, the lie, or malicious mental malpractice — says, "I can make you believe in both the beast and the false prophet, that is, I can make you believe in both materiality and false mentality." These two servants of the dragon stand for the whole of the apparent material universe. The beast is the belief in many material bodies, and the false prophet is the belief in many mortal minds.

These two symbols — many material bodies and many mortal minds — make up the sum total of outward manifestation through which the one evil, the dragon, or malicious mental malpractice, appears to operate. God, the one cause, always appears to us as manifestation, or effect; so in like manner, the dragon — the supposititious opposite of God — also seems to appear to us as manifestation, or effect. But through divine Science, we know that the supposition is never effect, is never a mind or body. It may appear as effect, but it is really always the same old dragon — a state of mental deception.

In our efforts to dispel the belief of malicious mental malpractice from our thought, we should not be misled into handling either the beast or the false prophet; that is, we should not handle either the physical or the false mentality. They are merely the supposititious opposites of God, or Mind. But we should handle the dragon, or the hypnotic suggestion that there is a physical body or a false mentality.

Our Active Duty

There is but one infinite Mind and one infinite body. The belief in many bodies means limitation and all that that term implies in the way of sin, sickness, age and death. The belief in many minds is the other aspect of the same belief in limitation, and results in many religions, many governments, many fears, and all forms of good and evil mentalities.

In this present age, the clearer vision of divine Science defines all evil as malicious mental malpractice. And because of this correct definition of evil, we are learning the deceptive character of all evil. When we fully understand that evil is always deceptive in character, then malicious mental malpractice is powerless to harm us. Evil is not a presence, a thing, a condition nor a person. It is merely a false mental picture, a caricature of mortal mind which does not exist.

Students, our own Mind, God, has given us dominion over all evil beliefs. Let us use our dominion. Our duty at this present time is not passive, but active. It seems that evil will defeat us in spite of all that we can do, but to be passive and just let things work out as they will, is not to reflect the active Life that is God, or to reflect that active dominion that is God. To be active in Truth is to establish our birthright as the son of God, which is freedom from all evil.

5. HEALING

Vital Christianity

Today, we are facing a world crisis in Christianity, just as we are facing a world crisis in democracy and freedom. Christian people throughout the world believe that Christianity is essential in saving the peoples of the world. They believe that the Christian religion is the hope of the world's civilization. But the theoretical Christianity of today is far removed from vital Christianity.

The Christian people who are awake to this world crisis in religion, are crying out for an active salvation, a living faith, a deeper understanding. There are more than 200 Christian religions founded on creeds and doctrines, besides hundreds of so-called heathen religions. But vital Christianity is not based on creeds and doctrines, nor is it necessarily found in lofty cathedrals.

Vital Christianity was made manifest in Christ Jesus. His life, his words, his works are our example, and we should follow him. The religion Christ Jesus founded, is vital Christianity. He taught it and practiced it. The principles that he advocated and lived were co-operative, benevolent, mutual, and all-inclusive. This vital Christianity as taught by Christ Jesus, concerned the relations between man and God, and between man and man. The law of this vital Christianity was called the Golden Rule, which reads, "Whatsoever ye would that men should do to you, do ye even so to them."

Today, there is much thought and investigation going on in the realm of religion, and according to the prophecy of Mrs. Eddy in *Pulpit and Press*: "Christ will give to Christianity his new name, and Christendom will be classified as Christian Scientists." Why will Christendom turn naturally to Christian Science? Because it is Science, because it is the impersonal Christ, or Truth. Christian Science is a vital, practical religion; it is a religion of works more than words. Christian Science, when better understood, will again "heal the sick, raise the dead, cleanse the lepers, cast out demons," as it did in the days of Christ Jesus.

The Healing Work Paramount

It is by keeping the healing work paramount that the world will be brought into the consciousness of the truth of Christian Science. It is the healing work that will prove to the world that the kingdom of good is within the individual consciousness. Through divine revelation, Mrs. Eddy knew that the salvation of the world would be brought about through the healing of sickness and sin.

Mrs. Eddy writes in the *Manual of The Mother Church*, "Healing the sick and the sinner with Truth demonstrates what we affirm of Christian Science, and nothing can substitute this demonstration." She continues, "I recommend that each member of this Church shall strive to demonstrate by his or her practice, that Christian Science heals the sick quickly and wholly, thus proving this Science to be all that we claim for it."

Students, healing the sick and the sinner is the sacred duty of each member of the Christian Science church. I am sure that Mrs. Eddy did not mean that each member should put his name in *The Christian Science Journal*. Just having our name in the *Journal* does not do the healing. Neither does not having our name in the *Journal* let us escape the sacred duty of healing the sick and the sinning.

Since each member of our church is to practice healing the sick and the sinning, where do we do this practice work? We always do it within the realm of our own individual consciousness. And where are the sick and the sinning that are to be healed? They are not outside or apart from us, they too are within the realm of our own mentality. What are the sick and the sinning "that Christian Science heals . . . quickly and wholly?" The sick and the sinning are not corporeal personalities that are to be changed and restored and healed. No! The sick and the sinning are a false, deceptive, mistaken sense — a distorted caricature of individual man — and we heal this false sense through our practice work of seeing man as he is in truth. Like Jesus, we are to behold "in Science the perfect man . . . where sinning mortal man appears to mortals." (*Science and Health*)

What is the attribute that is necessary in practicing Christian Science? Righteousness is the attribute necessary for our practice work. Each member of this church should purge, cleanse, and purify himself of the insistent mesmeric suggestion that there is someone who or something that needs to be healed or made whole. There is no righteous thought in the belief that the one we are helping is a human being doing something either right or wrong.

To heal "quickly and wholly" we must see that infinite God and His infinite manifestation constitutes our consciousness to the exclusion of all else. When we, in our practice work, have the "Christly affection" which wins our own pardon from the belief of life and intelligence in matter, and from the belief that man is personal, then we win the same pardon for the one we are helping.

Our textbook admonishes us: "Know thyself, and God will supply the wisdom and the occasion for a victory over evil." To know ourselves is a necessary requirement in our practice work. We should know ourselves as we are in Truth. We should know ourselves as individual man including the spiritual universe. We should know ourselves as a true state of consciousness, having the kingdom of heaven within. And as we know ourselves aright, we shall cease to know anyone or anything in our consciousness as imperfect or depleted. Then all men and all things will be to us as they are in the kingdom of heaven within us. Our textbook says, "It is indeed no small matter to know one's self," and many of us can testify to the truth of this statement.

Jesus gave the essential requirement for healing the sick and the sinning for all time. He said, "Physician, heal thyself." And again he said, "First cast out the beam out of thine own eye; and then shalt thou see clearly to cast out the mote out of thy brother's eye." When we see what we call another, we are seeing ourselves, for we can see and feel only what is in our own mentality. And as we heal ourselves of false mesmeric beliefs, we see our universe, which is within our mentality, as perfect and complete. And as we cast out the beam — that insistent, mesmeric caricature of infinite good — from our own eye, that is from our own consciousness, the mote that we thought we must remove from our brother's eye will have disappeared into its nothingness.

If we fail to demonstrate in our practice that Christian Science heals quickly and wholly — that is, if we are not seeing and feeling conscious Truth as all — then we need to enter our closet and there, alone with God — our own Mind — ask ourselves, "What is hindering me? Let the error in my thinking be uncovered." And then rise in the strength of Spirit to resist those mental foes — those insistent mesmeric suggestions — that we do not have sufficient understanding, that we do not know how to heal, that we do not really want this healing truth, and that we do not want to heal the sick and the sinning wholly and quickly.

Metaphysical Healing and Spiritual Healing

In Christian Science there are two kinds of healing — metaphysical healing and spiritual healing. Spiritual healing is the way Jesus healed and is the scientific method. Metaphysical healing is the spiritualization of our human thought, and constitutes our ascending footsteps up to where the spiritual healing is possible.

We read in *Science and Health* that "the letter and the mental argument" — that is, the affirmations of Truth and the denials of error — in and of themselves, do not do the healing work. These affirmations and denials "are only human auxiliaries to aid in bringing thought into accord with the spirit of Truth and Love, which heals the sick and the sinner."

We continue the mental arguments in our practice work until, like Jesus, we are able to heal instantaneously through Spirit alone. Today, the tendency is to have too much of the letter. There are so many wonderful statements given to us in our lessons, and lectures, and literature. We know they are scientific statements of Truth and we are overjoyed with them; but until we enter into "the secret place" and commune with these statements of Truth, individualize them, and be them actively and consciously, we do not have the power to heal the sick "quickly and wholly."

Students, we need more of the Christ consciousness within us, more of the awareness of divine Love wherein there is no evil, no practitioner, no patient, but wherein is only the presence of God, or Mind. Were we truthfully to appraise ourselves, there might be much hypocrisy found within us. We say one thing with our lips and believe another thing with our minds. We try to heal the human concept of man and things, when man and things are already perfect — "the same yesterday, and today, and forever." So often we make our affirmations and denials from the standpoint that Mind knows both good and evil, when God, the one Mind, our Mind, knows only good. And we do this unconscious of what we are doing.

All too often our healing work drops to the level of *materia medica*. We believe that our erroneous concept of man as a mortal material personality, is man separated from God and needing to be healed. But in true healing, we rise above this false concept of man into the stratosphere of Truth, wherein we behold the only man — "the perfect man" that Jesus beheld.

Our textbook teaches us that man "does not pass from matter to Mind, from the mortal to the immortal, or from good to evil. Such admissions cast us headlong into darkness and dogma" (*Science and Health* 244:25). Our textbook also teaches that we are not to try to heal our misconception of man, but to instantly recognize that "Now are we the sons of God." St. Paul said to the Ephesians: "Put off . . . the old man . . . and be renewed in the spirit of your mind; and put on the new man, which after God is created in righteousness and true holiness."

In our textbook, Mrs. Eddy has given us the chapter "Christian Science Practice" to help us in our healing work. In this chapter she not only sets forth the arguments — that is, the affirmations and denials — for the metaphysical treatment of every known trouble of mankind, but she also leads our thought on and up into the realm wherein the spiritual healing is accomplished. Students, whenever we are faced with physical or mental inharmonies, we should always turn to this chapter. It will answer our every need.

We should follow the simple directions in this chapter rigorously. For example, Mrs. Eddy says, "The physical affirmation of disease should always be met with the mental negation." Notice that she says "always" — not just sometimes. This requirement is so clear that anyone should be able to follow it. Again she says, "By lifting thought above error, or disease, and contending persistently for truth, you destroy error."

All Error is Mesmerism

No matter what the error is with which we are confronted, Mrs. Eddy says, "the counter fact relative to [this error] is required to cure it." The error is always mental, always a false mesmeric belief. It is never a thing, a person, nor a condition. It is always a hypnotic state of the so-called human mind, and we are to counter this hypnotic state with the Mind that is Truth.

The ancients saw a round earth as flat, and they believed what they saw and saw what they believed, and they greatly feared what appeared to be flatness and limitation. This mistaken mental picture was real to them, until the hypnotic or mesmeric fear and belief was broken by the truth, which they accepted in consciousness, that the earth was round. These ancients did not have to change a condition, they only had to yield up their hypnotic belief.

When our thought is hypnotized or mesmerized, this mental state is induced by the insistent and persistent suggestions that something is wrong with us or with our universe. Then our human mind concentrates its attention on these seeming conditions of sin, disease, age, pain, or lack, and holds them tenaciously in thought. These so-called wrong conditions are wholly within the realm of our own human mind, and are wholly our human mind seeing and feeling its own thought-forms. These seeming wrong conditions are wholly a hypnotic or mesmeric mental state, which we have accepted and dwelt upon, and this false mental state can be off-set only with the truth about man and the universe which we entertain in our thought. Our mental realm is the place where we de-mesmerize or de-hypnotize ourselves of these seeming erroneous conditions or erroneous thought-forms of sin, disease, age, pain, or lack.

An important factor in metaphysical healing is that in the final analysis of these seeming conditions, we are led to the conclusion that what appears to be sin, disease, age, pain, or lack is not the claim at all. With the ancients, flatness was not the claim. The earth did not have a condition of flatness. The claim was their false mesmeric belief in a flat earth, while the earth was eternally round. This mesmeric belief was so entrenched in the mentalities of these ancients that it not only limited them, but it caused them to put to death the first man who insisted that the earth was round.

So it is with our mesmeric belief in sin, disease, age, pain, or lack; they are not the claims which we are to heal. These mesmeric beliefs are so entrenched in our mentalities that not only do they limit us in all our activities, but also we tenaciously fasten these false conditions on our brother man and our universe of things. Sin, disease, age, pain, and lack are not facts or conditions to be dealt with at all. They are not the claim. The claim is that our mentality has become so mesmerized with these insistent and persistent false suggestions that we believe these false thought-forms are inevitable and do exist in fact. Our work is to handle and extinguish the basic claim — the mesmeric belief that man is not whole and perfect and complete now. And we handle and extinguish this claim of imperfect man with our understanding that God and man is one being, and that man consciously identifies God, his own Mind, for ever and ever.

Association Address of 1943

Christ Jesus was so conscious of things and conditions as they were in fact, that to him the false appearance or erroneous sense conditions were not facts to be dealt with, any more than the appearance of the horizon is a fact to be dealt with. Jesus, who healed spiritually, touched the bier, and what appeared to be a dead man proved to be an ever living man. To the man classified by mortals as blind, Jesus understandingly said, "Receive thy sight." He said to the man who appeared deaf, "hear," and to the man who appeared lame, "walk."

Jesus knew that man could see and hear and walk and live, because the one infinite divine consciousness that sees and hears and walks and lives could not express itself in a sense of reversion. In all his work, Jesus followed the rule that he established for us all, which reads: "Judge not according to the appearance, but judge righteous judgment."

Let us assume that I believe my lung has an inharmonious condition. My mind has accepted the insistent suggestions of inflammation, congestion, soreness, and has attached them to my lung. Now, the inflammation, congestion, and soreness are not conditions of my lung, but this whole seeming experience is so-called mortal mind seeing and feeling its own erroneous thought-forms that it, itself, is being. With the spiritual understanding I have, that conscious Life is the substance and being of what I humanly call a lung, I deny that inflammation, congestion, and soreness are connected in any way with the divine fact of lung, any more than flatness is connected with the round earth.

Our textbook tells us to "detach sense from the body, or matter, which is only a form of human belief." So, I obey my rule and detach the erroneous sense of inflammation, congestion, and soreness from my lung, and put them entirely in the realm of belief. And I affirm and claim for my lung all the spiritual qualities of divine Life, as health, wholeness, indestructible substance, and conscious harmonious being. I do not have to change a diseased lung into a perfect one. My lung is already as perfect as God is perfect.

But I replace my false mesmeric belief with true consciousness, wherein everything is already perfect.

Students, whenever evil seems to appear in our universe of thought, we no longer interpret this appearance as an evil condition, but we understand it is an imperfect apprehension of some spiritual fact. When the earth appeared flat to the ancients, this was not a condition of the earth, but was their imperfect apprehension of a round earth. When we behold so-called material things, we no longer interpret these things as material substance; but we understand them as our mistaken sense or false belief about the divine substance of Spirit. The appearance of man as material, is never a condition of fact, but is our misapprehension of man as Mind's expression.

We are master of every erroneous condition that appears in our consciousness when we clearly understand that it is not a condition of matter, but is a mesmeric state of thought, or is belief only, and we subdue these false beliefs by letting the divine Mind be active as our mind. As we do this our human mind is freed from its limitations, and we behold ourselves as the perfect expression of eternal Life, which is man's genuine measure. It is so needful that we keep uppermost in our thought the one great fact that "All is infinite Mind and its infinite manifestation," — man, perfect and eternal now.

THE POWER OF A DIVINE IDEA
Association Address of 1944

1. The Power of a Divine Idea ... 49

2. Woman ... 60

3. Practical Operative Christian Science ... 74

4, Spiritual Power ... 81

5. The Theology of Jesus ... 87

THE POWER OF A DIVINE IDEA
Association Address of 1944

Today I welcome you, in a larger, truer sense, not as human personalities, but as sons and daughters of God, as individual ideas of supreme good, as individual ideas of Life, Truth, and Love. Our coming together on these association days is not repetition in the usual sense. It is not just doing the same thing year after year. Each association day is a day of further revelations, of higher unfoldments in our human consciousness, of those things which are already spiritual facts. This should be to us an inspirational day — a day in which to progress both mentally and spiritually.

In each association there is at least one outstanding idea, which, if accepted in consciousness, will unfold and bless and heal us throughout the year. This right idea is a living, conscious, irresistible power which demonstrates itself, and works the works of God.

There have been many healings during the past year by those students in the association who have learned to "be still and know" that this right idea, or the Christ within his own consciousness, demonstrates itself. Last year quite a number of students who never miss their association, were unable to attend because of the high water situation. I have been asked many times during the year to review the first subject of last year's program, so you will find that to be the first subject on our program today. Many of you who have heard this paper, "The Power of a Divine Idea," will kindly bear with the repetition, I'm certain. Like the Master Teacher, all teachers of Christian Science offer higher revelations of truth to their students. So, throughout this work, I shall amplify, enlarge or elucidate the subject of the power of a divine idea when it is made active in the human consciousness.

1. THE POWER OF A DIVINE IDEA

The power of right or divine ideas that we see and feel today, will become clearer and more real tomorrow. We become increasingly conscious of the power of these ideas by the increasing use we make of them. The unfoldment in our human consciousness of the power of divine ideas is infinite and limitless in scope, since God is the light thereof. This divine power will continue to unfold throughout all eternity.

Never in all history has the so-called human mind expressed the qualities of Deity in such immeasurable degrees and in such concrete visible forms as at this present time. When correctly understood, the qualities of power, capacity, exactness, precision, coordination, etc., that are so outstanding in our world are all evolved by divine Mind, and are in the divine Mind only. Then the question arises, how can these divine qualities of power, and capacity, and coordination appear to us as destructive forces? It is because so-called mortal mind has translated these divine qualities and their functionings as destructive, and then sees and feels its own destructiveness objectified. Mortal mind is ignorant that God and man, His manifestation, is one inseparable being.

We are learning that all these destructive powers hidden in the blind forces of matter, when correctly understood, are divine powers that inhere only in Spirit. Through the understanding of Christian Science we are more and more translating all power and substance and action, as well as man and the universe, back into Spirit. It is through translation that the subjective qualities of Mind are revealed.

One Inseparable Being

The greatest thing that can possibly come to human consciousness has come to us in this present age. This greatest thing is the divine idea of God and what He is in manifestation, or man, as one being. This spiritual fact of being has existed from everlasting to everlasting. This spiritual fact, that God and His manifestation, man, is one inseparable being, has always existed in Principle, but was made visible in concrete form for the first time with the birth of Jesus.

We may make the statement in Christian Science that God and man is one inseparable being. "Principle and its idea is one," Mary Baker Eddy tells us in our textbook, *Science and Health with Key to the Scriptures*. These statements may mean much to us, or they may be mere words to us. This oneness of God and His manifestation, man, means that man alone can do nothing. It means that God alone, without man, can do nothing — not even exist. Whatever is done within the realm of the spiritual universe God alone, without man, does not do it. In fact, whatever is done, whatever the circumstance or event, God and man do it together as one inseparable being.

If there were such a thing as sin in the world, it would be God and man sinning as one inseparable sin. If there were such a thing as death in the world, it would be God and man as one inseparable being, dying and being death. Since we cannot attach sin and death to God, we cannot attach them to man, because God and man is one inseparable being. God without man cannot be immortal, but God and man as one inseparable being is immortal, is Life eternal. This powerful divine idea, that God and man is one inseparable being, active in human consciousness, is indeed our Saviour.

This revelation came to Mary's consciousness as the result of her self-conscious communion with the Holy Ghost, or Science of being, which was her Mind. The patriarchs and prophets discerned that this divine idea of spiritual power existed as a fact in God or Spirit, and believed that it would be expressed visibly in human consciousness in some future time and in some unknown manner.

Mary was the first to give concrete proof of the spiritual power of the divine idea of God and man as one inseparable being in the form of Christ Jesus. We, as Christian Scientists, will be ready to progress when we live our lives from the standpoint of the revealed truth that God and His manifestation, man, is one inseparable being, or is "I AM THAT I AM." This divine idea active in human consciousness is almighty power expressed humanly.

Isaiah's Vision of the Divine Idea

The prophet Isaiah appraised the appearing of the divine idea of God and His divine manifestation, man, as one inseparable being. When this idea appeared to Isaiah, he appraised it as "unto us a child is born." And immediately he appraised even the first faint appearing of this divine idea as being in the fullness and completeness of its divine character. He appraised this divine idea as "Wonderful, Counselor, The mighty God, The everlasting Father, The Prince of Peace."

If we, like Isaiah, recognized that even this first faint appearance of a right idea in our consciousness is the Almighty God, and is already full, complete, perfect, finished and permanent, the result would be amazing. How few of the infinite ideas that knock at the door of our human consciousness are recognized as the Almighty God, and are given admittance, and allowed to unfold in their completeness and perfection and permanence. I fear not many of them. They are forgotten almost immediately.

When Isaiah wrote the outstanding statement, "For unto us a child is born," this divine idea was far in advance of its tangible, concrete appearance in human consciousness. When Isaiah wrote this prophecy, he was not referring to a little babe lying in a manger; he was referring to a divine idea that already existed in Principle; he was referring to the eternal fact that God and His manifestation, man, is one inseparable being.

Isaiah visioned so-called human life as evolved from God, divine Principle, not from matter or personality. Isaiah visioned man, the infinite idea of God, as begotten of the one Principle of all being; he saw man as untouched by sin and death; he saw Deity, divine Mind, manifested; he saw God as the Son made visible; he saw the coincidence of the human with the divine. This, too, was the vision that was born of Mary's human consciousness by the Holy Ghost, or divine Science, and to which Mary gave concrete visible manifestation.

Isaiah visioned the joy in heaven and in earth when this mighty idea — God and His manifestation, man, as one inseparable being — would be presented in concrete form to the world, even though to material sense this divine idea appeared as a babe. Millions of babies had been born before this particular babe was born in the little town of Bethlehem, but not one of these millions had been heralded by an angel throng or a star in the East.

The Saviour, Christ Jesus

The Gospel of Luke records that an angel said unto the shepherds, "Fear not: for, behold, I bring you good tidings of great joy, which shall be to all people. For unto you is born this day in the city of David a Saviour, [an infinite idea], which is Christ the Lord." The angel did not say that a child was born, but he said a Saviour is born, and this Saviour is Christ the Lord, the divine idea, the living conscious irresistible truth of the oneness of God and man that makes all men free.

This was a remarkable event. Nothing like it had ever appeared on earth before. The narrative continues: "And suddenly there was with the angel a multitude of the heavenly host praising God [not praising a baby], and saying, Glory to God in the highest, and on earth peace, good will toward men." These angel visitants beheld not the human concept called a babe, but they beheld the concrete visible idea, the Saviour.

At this time, Caesar Augustus was ruler of the Roman empire and his supposed power and law was so great that he did as he pleased with the lives and the property of millions of people.

The Power of a Divine Idea

Never before had a mortal swayed such power, and never again will a mortal sway such power. Why? Because unto us has been born a divine idea, a Saviour. And when correctly appraised as Almighty God, this divine idea, or Saviour, in our human consciousness is irresistible power and law, which demonstrates itself.

When the hosts of heaven heralded the appearance of this divine idea — this Saviour, Christ the Lord — Caesar Augustus sensed there was being established on earth a permanent empire clothed with divine power and law, and that his seeming power and law would fade into its native nothingness.

To the shepherds Jesus was Immanuel. To them Deity had taken on the form of flesh and blood. But Mary's concept of man had risen above matter and material sense, and while others might see man as flesh and blood, Mary's idea of God was God's idea of Himself, the Christ. Mary's mode of consciousness was the Truth, the Christ, and she gave her true conception of man visible birth.

By reason of Mary's divine conception and its visible proof, she clearly understood that in every instance, whether it was sin, sickness, or death, Christ Jesus was to give to the world the proof of the supremacy of Spirit or Mind over matter or mortal mind. This was Jesus' mission in the world; and this is also our mission, as Christian Scientists, in the world today. We, too, are to give proof of the supremacy of Spirit or Mind over matter or mortal mind. And we do this as we understand that the divine idea is man, the Christ, and not a personality.

Immediate Evidence of the Divine Idea

"There was a marriage in Cana of Galilee; and the mother of Jesus was there." (John 2) It was at this wedding feast that Mary demanded of Jesus that he give proof or evidence of the power of Spirit or Mind over matter or mortal mind. Mary said to Jesus, "They have no wine." To their sense their supply of wine was exhausted. Indeed, Mary perceived that they had no wine, that is, no inspiration; they had no understanding with which to discern that the underlying fact of all visible things is inexhaustible. Mary demanded of Jesus that he give proof or evidence of this fundamental, operative, inexhaustible divine idea which is our Saviour from all want and lack.

Jesus said to his mother, "Mine hour is not yet come." But this was not Mary's sense of the divine idea. Had she not given visible proof of the invisible fact of God as Christ Jesus? Jesus, no doubt, had yet to ascend above the restrictions that material suggestions seemed to impose upon him.

Mary knew that there must be the human proof or evidence of the invisible, inexhaustible God or infinite good that underlies all visible things. She knew that evidence of this fact or divine idea must be in concrete, tangible, visible form at that very hour. She had the understanding and the absolute faith that God, Mind, the creative cause, is ever in operation, and of necessity must present His own ideas or evidences. Therefore, she could say unhesitatingly to the servants at the wedding feast, "Whatsoever he saith unto you, do it."

Jesus knew that a divine idea or spiritual inexhaustible fact was underlying the human sense of water, and because of this understanding he turned the human sense of water into wine — that is, he turned the limited sense into an inexhaustible sense, and the human sense of the guests was satisfied.

Any human sense of need is supplied by the divine idea or the spiritual inexhaustible fact underlying the need, and this fact or idea appears to us in the form that best satisfies our human sense. There is a divine idea or divine basis for everything that appears to us humanly.

At this wedding feast, it was demonstrated for all people throughout the ages that any human sense of need is supplied by the divine idea or the spiritual, inexhaustible fact underlying the need, and this fact or idea appears to us in the form that best satisfies our human sense of need, whether that sense of need is health, home, or business.

Christian Science teaches us that when we look beyond all mortal sense testimony, beyond all limitation, to Mind for the divine fact, we express it instantly. When we look for the fact of Mind, then Mind outlines itself as that fact to meet the present need. In other words, the supply appears spontaneously in the form that best satisfies our human sense of that reality. This coincidence of the divine fact and the human need is our Christ Jesus that is with us always. In Matthew we read, "And lo, I am with you alway, even unto the end of the world." Not a personal but an impersonal Saviour is with us unto the end of all sense of need. At the wedding feast, Mind, the Mind of Jesus, spake, and it was done. The water was wine, instead of water. Not an instant intervened between Mind as the inexhaustible, invisible fact and the visible evidence of that fact.

Ideas Must Become Tangible

Far too many useful and important ideas appear in our human consciousness and remain there merely as ideas. We fail to present these ideas in visible, tangible form. Every right divine idea that comes to our human consciousness is begotten of God or Mind, and should be recognized as Almighty God, who of necessity unfolds and presents His own ideas, and evidences them humanly, visibly, and at hand, according to the human sense of need.

Mrs. Eddy once said, "To affirm that which is true, is to assert its possibility." She also said, "By affirming that to be true, but which to all human reasoning or sight, seems not to be true at all, you can bring it to pass."

The power and the infinitude of Mind make every affirmation of Truth instantly available. When we affirm a fact, we are asserting or enforcing the possibility of that fact. By affirming that which is true, we can bring it to pass, because bringing it to pass is simply the cognition in our consciousness of that which already is.

Association Address of 1944

What a vision of success and achievement is unfolded in us when once we understand that God and man — good and its manifestation — is one inseparable being. What certainty and assurance come to us when we appraise even the first idea that appears in our consciousness as a divine inexhaustible fact, as the Almighty God, complete, finished, perfect, and permanent.

More and more should we demand of ourselves that we give proof of these fundamental operative divine ideas which are our Saviour. And as we put these divine ideas to work in our consciousness, we, too, shall see the coincidence of the human with the divine fact.

The star of the East symbolizes divine Science. It was the star of divine Science that guided the wise men to the birth of a more spiritual idea, even the Virgin-mother's immaculate conception and visible presentation of man's real being. It is so necessary that we let divine Science guide our thought to this true idea of God and man as one inseparable being, and that we accept and demonstrate this true idea in our daily lives. This true idea of God and man as one inseparable being will prove to be our Saviour from all personal sense — from all want, and age, and sin, disease, and death.

Angels

It is remarkable how often divine ideas and divine experiences appear in our human consciousness as angels. And how often we are unaware of them as being angels. In a general sense we think of angels as disconnected from God, and as external to our consciousness. But in truth or fact, angels are divine Mind's powerful impressions of good appearing in human consciousness.

Angels are as real as any other part of God's creation. It is the carnal mind in us that has classified man — the compound of divine ideas or experiences of good — as "a little lower than the angels." In the spiritual account of creation, man is represented as

The Power of a Divine Idea

God's grandest product. "God said, Let us make man in our image, after our likeness." Man was not made of a lower order; he was not made a "little lower than the angels." Man is the divine ideas, or divine experiences, or angels, as God created them. These powerful spiritual impressions of good that come to the human consciousness is man in the image and likeness of God.

The angels of the Lord, or these divine ideas or experiences of good, appear to us when our consciousness is prepared to receive them. Angels are Mind's messages — powerful impressions of good. They are truly mental and must be mentally received by us in our individual mentality. Angels, divine ideas or experiences of good, are exalted thoughts, healing truths, positive right convictions, that appear to us as our human thought.

These angel visitants come to us as a "still, small voice" within us; they come as a great enlightenment, as an unfoldment of truth; they come as a surprising thought or conviction, as just the right thing to say or to do. As a rule, angels come suddenly, but are always timely. They usually come as promptings or as restraining intuitions. Isaiah portrayed the appearing of angels to our mentalities when he wrote, "And thine ears shall hear a word behind thee, saying, This is the way, walk ye in it, when ye turn to the right hand, and when ye turn to the left."

To those mentalities in tune with the divine Mind, these angel visitants, divine ideas or experiences, are innumerable. They are the incidents of every hour, and are the privileged lot of every individual. Angels are the invisible essence and substance of our visible experiences. Through them the invisible appears visible in human consciousness. Angel messages, divine ideas or divine experiences, are invisible to human consciousness, but become externalized in a way that can be seen and understood. The angel Gabriel, representing the might of God, came invisibly to Zacharias. The old priest's mentality was so filled with the firm conviction that "with God all things are possible," that this truth externalized itself or was made visible to Zacharias, as his long-desired son, who later became John the Baptist. (See Luke 1:5-25.) Zacharias, whose whole heart's desire was that he might have a son, was earnestly striving after righteousness, the right thinking about God and man as one inseparable being. His mentality was in oneness with divine Mind, and it was quite natural that the angel, or divine idea of God's omnipotence, came as a sudden conviction that "with God all things are possible."

God's goodness is impartial. He does not withhold anything from us. "These angels of His presence" are something which we, in our ignorance, are withholding from ourselves. Miracles do not just happen. When we change our innermost thoughts to accord with the angels of His presence, this puts into operation spiritual law, which causes the externalization of that which from the beginning has already been bestowed.

2. WOMAN

This morning in our amplification of the power of a right idea — the idea of God and man as one inseparable being — we shall begin with the first faint gleam that came to human consciousness. The first faint gleam of the power of the divine idea, which is the Saviour of mankind, appeared in the consciousness of Eve in the Garden of Eden. And we shall follow the unfoldment in human consciousness of the almighty power of this divine idea or Saviour up to our present age, where it has culminated in its entirety as divine Science or Christian Science.

We who are awake to the truths of Christian Science know that no experience of which we are humanly conscious just merely happens. The sense of our human experience may be sadly awry, nevertheless everything of which we are conscious is in the order of divine Science.

Since everything is in divine order, it is quite enlightening and worthy of our consideration, that the seven successive fuller unfoldments of the Christ, the divine idea or our Saviour, were made visible to the world through seven women, portrayed in the Scriptures. These seven women who unfolded the Christ in human consciousness were:

1. Eve, called "the mother of all living."
2. Sarah, called "a mother of nations." Sarah was the mother of Isaac, a child of promise.
3. Miriam, a prophetess, who at the Red Sea sang the song of triumph for the supremacy of Spirit over matter and evil.
4. Deborah, called "a mother in Israel." A prophetess who said to Barak: "Up; for this is the day in which the Lord hath delivered Sisera into thine hand."
5. Ruth, the gentle gleaner, who said, " . . . thy people shall be my people, and thy God my God."

6. The Virgin Mary, who said of herself, " . . . for, behold, from henceforth all generations shall call me blessed."

7. The woman in the Apocalypse. Without doubt, the woman in the Apocalypse is typified by Mary Baker Eddy, who has given to the world the impersonal universal Christ in divine Science.

The Christ, or the divine idea of God and man as one inseparable being, could come only through woman — could come only through woman's receptive recognition of the fatherhood of God and the Scriptural sonship of man. The word *woman*, as used in the Scriptures, represents a type of consciousness.

Today, when speaking of these seven women, we would miss the mark entirely were we to think only of seven female personalities. The term *woman* as used in the Scriptures refers to modes of spiritual discernment, or to a purity of consciousness. The high spiritual quality of thought maintained by these seven women was the medium through which the divine messages from God were made visible to the world.

Today, since our time is limited, we shall consider only three of these seven women through whom the divine idea or Saviour has appeared — Eve, the Virgin Mary, and the woman in the Apocalypse, typified by Mary Baker Eddy.

Eve

Eve, the woman in the Garden of Eden, prefigured the coming of the Christ, or the divine idea of God and man as one inseparable being, which is our Saviour. Mrs. Eddy says Eve means a beginning. (See *Science and Health* 585:23-28.) Eve typifies an appearing or a beginning of a more righteous thought that came to the human consciousness to deliver mankind from evil.

The first faint gleam that the Christ, or Saviour, was not a personality, but was mental and spiritual in character, appeared in the consciousness of Eve in the Garden of Eden. And it has taken us a long time to discern that our Christ, or Saviour, is found wholly within our secret thought, and must be understood as the divine idea of God and man as one inseparable being.

As time passed on, this divine idea of the Christ, or Saviour, that first appeared to Eve became clearer, and finally became visible in concrete form as the babe Jesus, who grew into the spiritually mental stature of the power of Spirit, as Christ Jesus. And lastly in our day this divine idea of the Christ, or Saviour, this mode of righteous thought, has unfolded as the impersonal understanding of divine Science.

This first day of human awakening came to the consciousness of Eve when she faintly glimpsed the divine idea of God and man as one inseparable being. And the unfoldment in our consciousness of this same divine idea of God and man as one inseparable being is our Saviour, which will eventually lead us all to that seventh day of spiritual unfoldment, wherein this inseparable oneness is fully understood, and the serpent, or false sense, is cast into the "lake of fire," or into the consuming truth of God's infinitude.

In religious history, it is generally admitted that the woman Eve was not a human personality. This narrative of the Garden of Eden is a Scriptural allegory or a great religious fable. This fable and the lesson it taught were handed down from generation to generation to impress upon thought the distinction between good and evil, and the effects of good and evil. This fable was personified by Adam and Eve and the serpent in the Garden of Eden, and is a misstatement about God and His spiritual creation as set forth in the first chapter of Genesis.

The Garden of Eden, Adam and Eve, together with the serpent, all typify states or modes of consciousness. Eve was a mode of consciousness in which the spiritual idea of God and His creation had its beginning. When the truth appeared in the thought of Eve, this true spiritual sense enabled her to recognize the serpent, or the lie of personal sense, which she had accepted as her thought. Eve saw the contradictory natures of good and evil, and discerned the folly of believing that both were true.

The enmity of the serpent against the woman, specifically mentioned in the first and last books of the Bible, does not imply a radical discrimination between men and women. This enmity against woman, or the spiritual mode of consciousness, illustrates the antagonism of the carnal mind towards spirituality, whether found in the consciousness of man or woman.

This enmity between the serpent, personal sense, and woman, spiritual sense, is the inherent and irreconcilable conflict between the flesh and Spirit, or between the spiritual and sensual elements, or between truth and error in human consciousness.

The serpent, personal sense, and the woman, spiritual sense, are opposite modes of thought. On the side of the serpent, or personal sense, are all the debasing influences which impel mankind toward moral and spiritual corruption. On the side of the woman, or spiritual sense, is found every uplifting and regenerating influence that touches human consciousness. It is through spiritual sense, or spiritualized consciousness, typified by woman, that humanity finds deliverance from the subtleties of the serpent, or personal sense, and awakens to the true consciousness that God and man is one inseparable being.

A divine hope was born in Eden when human thought first became impressed with the distinction between good and evil. This divine hope was born when woman, the mode of righteous thought, recognized the claims of personal sense as something not to be admitted, but to be denounced and dispelled.

When Eve discovered she had been lured into a state of error through mesmeric subtlety spoken of as the serpent, she recognized somewhat the purity and spirituality of God's creation. And this germ of spiritual awakening in human consciousness increased, and will continue to increase until it displaces all sense of evil in every human consciousness, and the seventh day, or the light of divine Science, unfolds in its fullness.

Mrs. Eddy, in speaking of the woman, says: "Truth, cross-questioning man as to his knowledge of error, finds woman the first to confess her fault. She says, 'The serpent beguiled me, and I did eat;' as much as to say in meek penitence, 'Neither man nor God shall father my fault.' She has already learned that corporeal sense is the serpent. Hence she is first to abandon the belief in the material origin of man and to discern spiritual creation. This hereafter enabled woman to be the mother of Jesus and to behold at the sepulcher the risen Saviour, who was soon to manifest the deathless man of God's creating. This enabled woman to be first to interpret the Scriptures in their true sense, which reveals the spiritual origin of man." (*Science and Health*)

The Virgin Mary

From the very moment that Isaiah uttered the prophecy, "Hear ye now, O house of David; . . . the Lord himself shall give you a sign; Behold, a virgin shall conceive, and bear a son, and shall call his name Immanuel," every daughter of Israel not only longed to become the mother of "the anointed," but thought it possible that she might become that mother. Therefore Mary, in common with other Jewish maidens of her period, cherished the hope of becoming the mother of the long-expected deliverer of Israel.

History tells us that the world of Mary's day was drowning in its foully materialistic thinking. Rome, the most important city, had set up the worship of the Emperor, the adoration of a human personality, as her religion. In the province of Galilee, where Mary lived, there were many established religions, and political parties — the Pharisees, the Sadducees, the scribes, the lawyers, and the revolutionists — all awaiting the hour to strike Rome.

The conception held by these groups concerning the deliverance of Israel was a wholly material conception. What remained of the morality and spirituality of the Israelites was at this time found only among the common people; and sacred history tells us that in this province of Galilee, and among the common people, was a little group of metaphysical thinkers. Right in the midst of this dense materialistic thinking of the upper class was this little group, a remnant of Israel, who practiced pure and undefiled religion. They taught and practiced the most beautiful moral precepts. In fact, they were full of light in that black night of materialism. Many of the literary productions nearest the advent of Jesus were written by these religious thinkers.

This little remnant of Israel was not discouraged concerning Israel's deliverance. Their faith in God was unshaken by the bloody ravages of Rome. They worshiped the true God; and of all the religions of that day, none approached the Hebrew religion in purity of doctrine or cleanness of life, as shown forth by this little group of metaphysicians.

The greater portion of this province of Galilee — the Pharisees, the Sadducees, the scribes, the lawyers, and the revolutionists — all looked for a materialistic deliverer to save them from the Roman Emperor. But this remnant of Israel, this group of metaphysicians, looked for a deliverer who would purify his people. They realized that Israel's woes were the result of her false and unrighteous thinking. Hence this little group looked for a spiritual king, who would deliver Israel from its materialistic mode of thought.

According to prophecy, their deliverer must belong to the highest order of being. He was to be called "Wonderful, Counselor, The mighty God, The everlasting Father," and he was to be born of a virgin of the family of David. His mission would be the salvation of his people and of all mankind. To him would be given everlasting dominion, glory, and a kingdom, and all people would serve him. (See Dan 7:14.)

To the Hebrew, his belief in prophecy was wholly beyond the interpretation of man. His beliefs were deeply entrenched in his thought. They had been prophesied by patriarchs and prophets, and handed down as fixed spiritual and mental laws of thought. To the Hebrews, prophecy was a fixed fact; and, too, they had demonstrated so many amazing experiences that they were confident that a spiritual deliverance would also be their experience. Since this prophecy was a fixed law to this little remnant of Israel, they made themselves ready for the coming promised deliverer. They purified their thought and made many marvelous demonstrations which logically followed their spiritual thinking. This little group knew from actual experience that spiritual law set in motion by purified, spiritualized thought was far more effective than the forcing of political issues through material aggression or human will.

Mary belonged to this group. So naturally her vision of the deliverer or Saviour of Israel was far from that of a mere political restorer who would set up in material splendor the ancient throne of David. Mary knew that this deliverer, or Saviour of Israel, who was awaited not only by Israel but by the whole world, must be one who would demonstrate Israel; that is, one who would set forth the real man in the image of Spirit. Mary realized that nothing short of a virgin conception, or a deep purity of thought, could bring into human visible form, a being who, for the task before him, must be spiritually endowed as no human being had ever been endowed before.

Mary was deeply religious, a woman of strong character and super-intelligence. She was far from the 'clinging vine' type to which so many have ignorantly assigned her. It is interesting and wonderful to learn how Mary, within herself, prepared for the coming of the Saviour. She was familiar with the Scriptures and knew that a virgin conception would not just happen. She knew that a virgin conception could take place only if the purity of the virgin's thought was sufficiently demonstrated.

Mary knew that the angel of the Lord, the divine idea, the reality of being, could come to the virgin's human consciousness in concrete visible demonstration only when that consciousness was prepared and ready both mentally and spiritually. She knew and understood the spiritual law that made invisible spiritual facts become humanly and materially visible to mankind.

Mary was familiar with the miracles of the ancient patriarchs and prophets. She clearly understood why the burning bush was not consumed. She understood, in some measure, how "Enoch walked with God: and he was not; for God took him." She knew why the pot of oil failed not, and how Elisha's own mind could say, "Thus saith the Lord, They shall eat, and shall leave thereof." She no doubt understood how and why the temple was rebuilt by King Cyrus; how and why there was rebuilding of the wall in Jerusalem under Nehemiah.

Mary no doubt prayed and sang the songs of David. To her, the Psalms were the same source of comfort and consolation as they have been to both Christian and Jew alike, down through the ages. Mary knew and understood the demonstration of Zacharias and Elizabeth, and she had seen many more demonstrations of spiritual import wrought out into concrete visible expression.

Mary knew that with God, her own Mind, all things were possible. She knew that in all these experiences the might of God or Mind came to the human consciousness as powerful impressions of good, and then these mental, spiritual impressions were externalized to mankind in concrete visible forms.

Mary knew that all things, circumstances, conditions, and events do not just happen. She clearly understood that any thought held in the mentality tends to express or externalize itself in outward or visible form. Therefore, Mary firmly believed that the longing and the undaunted faith in the certain coming of Israel's deliverer would some time become externalized.

Mary knew that if she, a virgin, were to become the mother of the Saviour, this demonstration could only be made through her spiritual understanding of the fatherhood of God. Her demonstration made, then indeed God would be the Father of her child, and her child would truly be the Son of God.

The annunciation, as recorded by Luke, was Mary's announcement to herself and to those who looked for Israel's deliverer that she was to be the mother of the Saviour who would save

The Power of a Divine Idea

not only Israel of that day, but all generations to come. This annunciation represents Mary's own reasoning; her communion with the angel was her communion with her own inner self. In a larger sense, her annunciation was her communion with God, her own Mind. This indeed was the power and operation of the divine idea in human consciousness.

In this annunciation, recorded in the Gospel of Luke, "Mary said, My soul doth magnify the Lord, and my spirit hath rejoiced in God my Saviour. For he hath regarded the low estate of his handmaiden: for, behold, from henceforth all generations shall call me blessed. For he that is mighty hath done to me great things; and holy is his name. And his mercy is on them that fear him from generation to generation." This annunciation by the Virgin Mary is the greatest poem in Hebrew literature. I will say it is the greatest poem that has ever been written.

Since Mary herself was of the royal lineage, she knew that God would give to her son the throne of David. Mary named her son Jesus, because Jesus was synonymous with Joshua, a renowned leader of Israel, and Mary's son would indeed be a leader. The name Jesus also comes from the Greek form of Je-hosh-ua, which means Jehovah saves. And why should Mary not attach to her son those qualities which in sacred history were promised to the Son of God?

When the angel — that mighty impression of good — appeared to Mary and said unto her, "The Holy Ghost shall come upon thee, and the power of the Highest shall overshadow thee: therefore also that holy thing which shall be born of thee shall be called the Son of God," Mary answered this angel saying, "Be it unto me according to thy word."

False theology has made the world believe that this statement made by Mary to the angel was made in a spirit of mere pious resignation on her part, and that Mary had little or at least very little to do with giving a Saviour to the world. But since the "Key to the Scriptures" has unlocked for us the Science of Mind, Mary's statement, "Be it unto me according to thy word," reveals Mary's thought as being on a lofty plane of spiritual power and realization. This statement is a confident assertion that nothing — not even the bringing forth of Israel's deliverer — was impossible with God. Her words were the acknowledgment of spiritual law.

A fundamental law has been revealed to us. This law is that *things do not merely happen*. Thought held persistently within our mentality tends toward the externalization of itself in outward and visible forms. The thought of the whole Hebrew nation, a thought born in the Garden of Eden, lay back of Jesus, the Saviour, and forced him into view.

The Virgin Mary's state of mind was the mighty God, the law of divine Science. This law, set in motion in the consciousness of Mary, gave us a Saviour who saves us from all sin, disease, age, want, war, and death. This law, active in the consciousness of Mary, gave visible proof that the Father of man was not a material personality, but was an all-creative Principle, known to Israel as their God.

Let us review some of the vital points in this lesson:

1. The divine idea or spiritual fact held persistently within the mentality will externalize itself in outward and visible forms.

2. The divine idea when correctly understood as the mighty God, or as active, powerful, conscious good, holds within itself the power to demonstrate itself.

3. Things do not merely happen. There is a divine basis for every human thing, circumstance, condition and event.

4. It is spiritual law, active in human consciousness, that causes spiritual facts to become humanly and materially visible to mankind.

5. The divine idea, or Saviour, will come to our human consciousness in concrete visible demonstration, only when our consciousness is prepared and ready, both mentally and spiritually.

The Power of a Divine Idea

The Woman In The Apocalypse

Through the woman in the Apocalypse, St. John the Revelator portrays a greater vision, a brighter light of understanding, a higher spiritual thought process, than was portrayed even by the spiritualized thought of the Virgin Mary.

Jeremiah in his day prophesied concerning the spiritual thinking that was to come. He said, "The Lord hath created a new thing in the earth, A woman shall compass a man." By this he meant that the inspired woman-thought would finally grasp the full wonder of God's man, and would demonstrate this real man in human consciousness.

And Jesus, in his day, prophesied that spiritual thinking, or a higher understanding of the divine idea, would appear in the human consciousness as the "Comforter." He said, "I will pray the Father, and he shall give you another Comforter, that he may abide with you for ever; even the Spirit of truth; . . . for he dwelleth with you, and shall be in you." And Mrs. Eddy in her day further enlightens by saying in *Science and Health*, "This Comforter I understand to be Divine Science."

St. John's Apocalyptic vision completes the beautiful picture of woman's place in prophecy. This vision completes the seventh day of unfoldment of spiritual thinking. To St. John "There appeared a great wonder in heaven; a woman clothed with the sun, and the moon under her feet, and upon her head a crown of twelve stars . . . And she brought forth a man child, who was to rule all nations with a rod of iron: . . . and behold a great red dragon . . . stood before the woman . . . to devour her child . . . And to the woman were given two wings of a great eagle, that she might fly into the wilderness . . . where she is nourished for a time . . . And the great dragon was cast out." (Revelation)

In this vision St. John presents spiritual thinking typified as "a woman clothed with the sun." This divine idea, or spiritual thinking typified by woman, is pictured as radiant with the light of spiritual understanding, with matter under her feet, and crowned with a diadem of victory. This divine idea, or spiritual thinking typified by woman, appears in this Apocalyptic vision in the fullness of spiritual understanding.

In this vision the woman brought forth a man child. Woman, portrayed as the fullness of spiritual understanding, brought forth Christian Science, which is to rule all nations with a rod of iron. Error, typified by the great dragon, resists this revelation. In other words, the spiritual sense of Life, Truth and Love, appearing as Christian Science, is confronted by the dragon, or serpent of personal sense.

But the divinely illumined consciousness, or woman-thought, is given two wings of a great eagle; she is given the understanding of the omni-action of conscious Life, with which she flies into the wilderness. And in *Science and Health*, Mrs. Eddy defines "wilderness" as "the vestibule in which a material sense of things disappears, and spiritual sense unfolds the great facts of existence."

Mrs. Eddy speaks of this woman in our textbook. She says, "The woman in the Apocalypse symbolizes generic man, the spiritual idea of God; she illustrates the coincidence of God and man as the divine Principle and divine idea."

Again, woman, typifying spiritual thinking, appears in John's Apocalyptic vision. This time she is seen in "a great and high mountain" as "the bride, the Lamb's wife." The Lamb's wife is the Word of God understood and demonstrated. The Lamb's wife is Christian Science, which explains and presents and demonstrates the Christ method of healing.

It is through the application in individual consciousness of Christian Science — this Comforter prophesied us by Jesus — that the works done by Christ Jesus are repeated. "The blind receive their sight, and the lame walk, and the lepers are cleansed, and the deaf hear, the dead are raised up, and the poor have the gospel preached to them."

Let us now consider our beloved Leader, Mary Baker Eddy. Without doubt Mrs. Eddy typifies the woman in the Apocalypse.

The Power of a Divine Idea

That is, Mrs. Eddy typifies or embodies all the characteristics of the pure woman-thought that was portrayed in St. John's vision. Mary Baker Eddy showed forth, or prefigured, or exemplified the spiritual consciousness portrayed in that great vision, and presented that spiritual consciousness to the world in concrete visible form as divine Science.

Mary Baker Eddy stands for something far greater than a good personality or a great human being. When correctly estimated, she stands for the complete revelation of Christ in the human consciousness. She stands for egoistic consciousness, the revealed Christ.

The Virgin Mary perceived the Christ and presented the Christ to the world through Jesus. But this was not enough. One more step must be taken. A positive rule must be given to humanity by means of which all mankind could demonstrate the Christ.

Science and Health with Key to the Scriptures, given to the world through Mary Baker Eddy's perception of this Christ, explains divine Science, or the Comforter, prophesied by Jesus and is leading humanity into all truth. Mrs. Eddy received the Christ, Truth, into her consciousness, and then gave this Christ, Truth, to us in her writings. Nothing further is required to guide us into all truth. We look for Mrs. Eddy in her writings where the revealed Christ is to be found.

St. John in his Revelation tells us, "And I saw another mighty angel come down from heaven . . . And he had in his hand a little book open." Mrs. Eddy tells us that this little book in the hand of the angel, and *Science and Health*, are one and the same. She refers to this little book in our textbook, where she named it "Truth's volume."

The truth that we have today is the same truth that unfolded in the Garden of Eden in the consciousness of Eve. It appeared in a much fuller degree in the spiritual thinking of the Virgin-mother. And this same truth has come to us as a full complete divine Science through the purity of our beloved Leader. This revelation of divine Science given to the world by Mary Baker Eddy did not just merely happen; like the Virgin-mother, Mary Baker Eddy prepared herself for this divine mission. She tells us in our textbook that she "won [her] way to absolute conclusions through divine revelation, reason, and demonstration."

Mrs. Eddy spent three years in the study of the Bible. After this intensive study of the Scriptures, in order to discover and understand spiritual law, she put her findings to a severe test by healing the sick and the sinning, and raising the dying to life and health. After this intensive preparation which covered a period of years, she published *Science and Health with Key to the Scriptures*, which will stand the test of the ages. *Science and Health* is Mrs. Eddy's revelation of provable spiritual law.

Through the reading of *Science and Health* thousands upon thousands have been healed of sickness and sin and have been enabled to live happy and useful lives. Is it any wonder that Christian Scientists love and revere their Leader? Is it any wonder that we are deeply grateful to her for the revelation of divine Science?

Mrs. Eddy fulfilled Scriptural prophecy. In this age she has brought to us the true meaning of the woman-thought in St. John's Apocalyptic vision. This woman-thought is divine Science and Mrs. Eddy speaks in the textbook of this woman-thought, or pure consciousness, as "Truth's immortal idea . . . sweeping down the centuries, gathering beneath its wings the sick and sinning."

3. PRACTICAL OPERATIVE CHRISTIAN SCIENCE

Today there is a world crisis in religion. Many deep thinkers regard our long-established religions as devoid of spiritual power. They feel that many churches should be classified as the angel in Revelation classified the church of the Laodiceans when he said: "Because thou art lukewarm, and neither cold nor hot, I will spue thee out of my mouth. Because thou sayest, I am rich, and increased with goods, and have need of nothing; and knowest not that thou art wretched, and miserable, and poor, and blind, and naked."

Thinking persons realize that we need more than fear or force or even goodwill based on better business, to save the post-war world. They firmly believe that a religion based on practical Christianity is the only hope of civilization. Christian people who are awake to this world crisis in religion are crying out for an operative Christianity, for an active practical salvation, for a living faith, for a deeper understanding of God and of themselves. They are crying out for divine theology that was made manifest through Jesus.

Are we awake to the fact that multitudes will come to Christian Science for help at the close of this great world struggle? Why will they come? They will come because of the full-orbed promise that they will find healing and restoration of both mind and body. And when the test for the fulfillment of this promise comes, let it not be said of Christian Scientists that "Thou art weighed in the balances, and art found wanting."

A Definite Life-purpose

Mrs. Eddy records her life-purpose. She says: "My life-purpose [is] to impress humanity with the genuine recognition of practical, operative Christian Science." And she further says to us,

"Drink with me the living waters of the spirit of my life-purpose." (See *Miscellaneous Writings* 207:1-6.)

There was no doubt in Mrs. Eddy's mind that she had a definite purpose in life to fulfill, and what this divine purpose was. No matter what others might do, this divine purpose was definitely fixed and established in her thought; and she knew she must follow this definite direction in life in order to fulfill her divine purpose, and give to humanity a visible proof of a practical operative Science when applied to human affairs.

When we recognize the magnitude of her purpose, the far-reaching results of the fulfillment of this purpose, what it has meant in our lifetime to have an unfailing ever-operative Science to apply to our human affairs, and when we realize that even a greater unfoldment will come to future generations, we may well marvel and express our gratitude for this blessing that has appeared to us in our world.

Jesus, too, was keenly aware that he had a definite purpose in life to fulfill. In answer to Pilate's question, he said, "To this end was I born, and for this cause came I into the world, that I should bear witness unto the truth."

Both Jesus and Mrs. Eddy had a clear sense of the significance of their so-called human experience. They recognized that no one was ever born out of due time. They knew that they had a definite purpose to fulfill, and they knew that they had the power and intelligence from God with which to fulfill that purpose.

Are we, as Christian Scientists, awake to the fact that we too have a definite life-purpose? And are we following a definite direction in life in order to fulfill this divine purpose? Today, as never before, we need to recognize the significance and value of the existence of each individual. We should watch and not become mesmerized with the seeming lack of value that is placed on the individual at this present hour. We should not just close our eyes and permit our thought to stand dormant concerning this lack of appreciation for human existence.

Let us bear in thought that there is nothing external to our own consciousness. Our own mind sees and feels its own projected thought. Our own mind does not see or feel another outside itself, or other than itself or unlike itself. When we see another, we are seeing ourselves. We see and feel only the contents of our own mind. St. Paul, in speaking to the Romans, said, "Wherein thou judgest another, thou condemnest thyself; for thou that judgest doest the same things."

In order to fulfill our definite purpose and to be a visible witness for Truth, we should be keenly aware of our individual existence in its higher spiritual aspects. We should be deep thinkers, we should vision happier days for the human family. We should prove that an abundant practical life is the one eternal life at hand. We should participate in, and rejoice in the present fulfillment of this vision, of this present liberating dispensation — the dispensation of the coming of the Son of man — which is the reality of all things being made visible in human consciousness.

As individual Christian Scientists we need a greater love for God and a greater love for man in our hearts, in order that our sublime life-purpose may be carried out into effect. Each of us has a sublime task to perform. We should so live and so love that God or Truth is made comprehensible to us and that we may hear His voice saying, "This is the way, walk ye in it."

Impressing Humanity with Practical Results

What does it mean to impress humanity with practical, operative Christian Science? The word 'practical' means that which is available, usable or valuable when in operation. The word 'operative' means the quality of action. It means to have the power of action which will produce results. "The term Christian Science relates especially to Science as applied to humanity," writes Mrs. Eddy. Then "practical, operative Christian Science" means a Science that is available to human consciousness, and is active in the production of results when applied practically and intelligently to human affairs.

Jesus, as the reflection or evidence of Mind, had no action, ability or power underived from God. His action, ability and power were God's action, ability and power ever operative as practical results. Jesus imparted to and impressed humanity in a practical way throughout his everyday experiences with what the Father-Mind revealed of Himself to him. He healed the sick, fed the multitude, opened the eyes of the blind, unstopped the deaf ears, provided the tax money, and raised the dead. Surely such deeds were the active and practical results of his divine theology within himself.

Mary Baker Eddy, too, as the reflection or evidence of Mind, had no action, ability or power underived from God. It was God's action, ability and power that impressed Mrs. Eddy in a practical way with what the Father-Mind revealed of Himself to her as Christian Science. And she demonstrated this Science through her daily living and experiences, healing the sick and raising the dead, and by committing to the pages of a book her sublime discovery. This indeed was impressing humanity with a practical, operative Christian Science. So, each one of us, as the reflection and evidence of Mind, has no action or power underived from God. We are the action, ability and power that God is being in manifestation, and this action, ability and power that God is being in manifestation, is ever operative in producing results.

It should be our purpose to impart to and impress humanity with what our Father-Mind has revealed of Himself to us of divine Science, and demonstrate this Science in our daily lives and experiences. We have the ability and power from God with which to impress humanity with what divine reason, revelation and demonstration have given us.

No matter how circumscribed our sphere in life may be, we have within ourselves a definite direction to follow, and a divine purpose to fulfill.

There never has been a time in the history of Christian Science when Christian Scientists need so clearly to hear the within voice of Truth, and to know there is nothing external or outside of their own consciousness. Within our individual self is the battlefield, and there too is found the victory. We need to watch our thought that it does not become confused with the issues of the day. We need to be spiritually keen and alert in our thinking. We need to be "undisturbed amid the jarring testimony of the material senses" and prove that Science is "still enthroned."

The Coming of the Son of Man

At this hour humanity stands at the threshold of a mental overturning, an overturning unparalleled in human history. Jesus prophesied this hour. He said there would be "upon the earth distress of nations, with perplexity." Then followed his prophecy of encouragement and hope in these words: "And then shall they see the Son of man coming in the clouds with great power and glory. And then shall he send his angels, and shall gather together his elect from the four winds, from the uttermost part of the earth to the uttermost part of heaven." (Mark 13)

This prophecy of Christ Jesus, interpreted according to Christian Science, means far more than is seen on the surface. What is the coming of the Son of man?

The Son of man is not a person, but is the expression of the God-Mind in its totality of life, substance, and intelligence. These expressions of life, substance, and intelligence appearing in the highest sense comprehensible to human consciousness, is the coming of the Son of man.

The prophecy reads, "Then shall he send his angels." This means that God or Mind will send His messages, His mighty mental and spiritual impressions, into the hearts of men at this time, just as He did to the patriarchs and prophets, to Zacharias, to Mary, to the Revelator, and to Mary Baker Eddy, if we are prepared to receive them and desire these saving messages as they did.

These angels are the God-Mind made comprehensible, practical, and visible in the human consciousness of this day. Who can doubt that many are the saving angels that come to men on the battlefield, on the sea, in the air, as well as to the business man, and to the wife or mother in the home, when they in their thinking reach out to God as their only deliverer?

The prophecy reads, He "shall gather together his elect from the four winds, from the uttermost part of the earth to the uttermost part of heaven." God's elect are not persons, are not saints, are not even those who classify themselves as Christian Scientists. No. The elect are God's revelations of Himself, revelations of His life, His substance, His intelligence, appearing in our individual experiences. Life, substance, and intelligence are God's essential qualities or revelations, and are His elect.

God or Mind reveals Himself in His essential quality of life, which gives to God, man, and everything in the universe, the sense of eternal existence. God or Mind reveals Himself in His essential quality of indestructible substance, which gives to God, man and everything in the universe the eternal sense of dimension or sense of filling space. God or Mind reveals Himself in His essential quality of intelligence, which gives to God, man and everything in the universe the conscious qualities of feeling, knowing, and being.

At this time, God's elect — conscious life, conscious substance, and conscious intelligence, as they are in reality — are appearing in fuller and clearer degrees in our human experience. These spiritual and omnipotent operations of God or Mind, typified by the four winds, is the spiritual understanding that is coming to the human consciousness. This spiritual understanding is coming universally and practically, and is the coming of the Son of man.

Wherever these spiritual and omnipotent operations of God appear in human consciousness — even though in a limited degree, or in the uttermost parts of the earth — right there in that place, God or Mind is gathering together in unity His elect — His infinite qualities of life, substance, and intelligence, as they are in reality — and He is lifting them up to the uttermost parts of heaven, or is lifting these qualities in human consciousness to their highest degree of reality.

The Power of a Divine Idea

Are we, under whatever circumstances, looking within? Are we letting the divine understanding reign and be all? Are we comprehending, and experiencing eternal Life concretely? Are we experiencing the substance of God that is free from all discord and decay? Is our intelligence the pure consciousness of God without restrictions and limitations? If we, as Christian Scientists, are experiencing in some degree these qualities in our daily living, then we have a practical, operative Christianity.

4. SPIRITUAL POWER

Spiritual power does not just happen to come to us. Spiritual power is forever at hand, but it appears to us only as we put off the material sense of life.

It is natural for us, at times, to long for the quiet days of the past. And some Christian Scientists are content to remain in the same old mental and material grooves. So-called mortal mind tenaciously resists stir and change. Nevertheless progress or higher unfoldment in any field of endeavor, whether economic, educational, or metaphysical, is not made without launching out into newer and higher modes of thought.

In order to gain spiritual power and fulfill our divine purpose in life, we must prepare our thought. We must educate mortal mind out of itself by bringing every wrong thought in our mentality into captivity, into obedience to Christ, Truth.

Mrs. Eddy spent many years in study, and in the healing of incurable diseases, before she gave to the world *Science and Health*. Both Mrs. Eddy and Jesus learned to *do* by *doing*, and learned to *be* by *being*.

Mrs. Eddy sets forth inescapable requirements by which we prepare our thought and gain that higher understanding which gives us spiritual power. For example, in *Retrospection and Introspection*, she says, "thought must be spiritualized, in order to apprehend Spirit. It must become honest, unselfish, and pure, in order to have the least understanding of God in divine Science." This is an emphatic admonition that we as Christian Scientists need to heed.

Spiritualization Through Translation

What is the process through which thought is spiritualized? Mrs. Eddy tells us the process is "the translation of man and the universe back into Spirit." Through translation, we exchange our mode of material thought about man and the universe for a mode of spiritual thought that is the fact of man and the universe. In so doing, we become the spiritual fact of man and the universe. We should take our Concordances and gain a clear understanding of the word 'translation.' Our progress spiritward depends upon the translation of matter into Mind. (See *Miscellaneous Writings* 25:12; 74:15.)

Mrs. Eddy makes the following statement in our textbook, "The compounded minerals or aggregated substances composing the earth, the relations which constituent masses hold to each other, the magnitudes, distances, and revolutions of the celestial bodies, are of no real importance, when we remember that they all must give place to the spiritual fact by the translation of man and the universe back into Spirit." Why are these things of no real importance? Because we do not see these things as they are in fact. We see only our material concept of them. Mortal mind or the lie has classified these spiritual ideas as matter or objects of material sense, and we, through immortal Mind, must translate the material objects back into their originals until we see them as divine facts.

Let us be honest. How many of us, a few weeks ago, translated the eruption of Mount Vesuvius and its rocks back into originals, back into divine ideas, perfect and eternal as Mind? Our textbook says, "Spiritually interpreted, rocks and mountains stand for solid and grand ideas." How many of us translated the hidden, blind, destructive forces of matter that were attached to Vesuvius back into their originals — back into the almighty forces that inhere in Spirit only?

So-called mortal mind says that the hidden destructive forces attached to Vesuvius are the destructive forces attached to our world today, are remote and apart from us, and over there. 'Over there' is always here. The so-called mortal mind that is over there is the same mortal mind that is here. The same destructive forces that seem to be over there are here within the realm of our own individual mind. Perhaps the degree is not the same, but the quality is the same.

Association Address of 1944

Unless we, through our own immortal, divine Mind, translate these seeming destructive forces back into their originals, back into the omnipotence, omniscience, and omnipresence of the divine Mind, we shall continue to see and feel mortal mind's thought objectified. It is only through translation that we lose the material sense of things and our thought becomes spiritualized.

To what extent are we translating ourselves, our bodies and their so-called functionings, back into their originals — back into divine ideas and divine functionings? Mortal mind has classified us as matter and has given us a material sense of body and its functionings. But through translation, immortal Mind gives us the original, gives us man in God's image and likeness, gives us body as Mind's embodiment of right ideas, gives us functions as the perpetual operations of Mind forever eternal and harmonious.

When we translate the objects of material sense, the things of our universe, ourselves, our bodies and their functionings, into their originals, we do not deal with anything external or objective to ourselves. No. We replace the material sense object and its operations with divine ideas, and we do the replacing wholly within the realm of our own thought. This is the process through which our thought becomes spiritualized, so that we may apprehend Spirit.

The universal belief that ideas have become material things is the fundamental lie. What any material thing may seem to do or be is a lie about the eternal fact at hand. What is called a material body, or a material mountain, or a world war, or a poor business, is a false human concept of a divine idea at hand. It is the belief that ideas have become material and that man must have life and consciousness through the medium of matter. Through translation, we can gain our freedom from false beliefs and experience the divine facts in their reality.

Mrs. Eddy says of Christ Jesus, "His earthly mission was to translate substance into its original meaning, Mind." She also says, "The great difficulty is to give the right impression, when translating material terms back into the original spiritual tongue."

The Power of a Divine Idea

In order to give the right impression when we translate material terms back into the original spiritual tongue, we must grasp the spiritual sense of the original. Could any of us be affected by altitude if we knew we include within ourselves the spiritual fact, the only fact of altitude? The mountain, the grand and lofty idea of God, is not outside of us or apart from us, but it is part of the compound of ideas that is us.

Through translation of man and the visible universe back into the spiritual fact of man and the universe, we shall finally see and know that an elephant, or a planet, or airplane, is not larger or mightier than ourselves. We shall see all things as thought-forms or ideas or spiritual facts included within us and as possessing all the qualities and attributes of God.

As Christian Scientists we are to grasp the spiritual sense of the originals. The spiritual originals can only be discerned spiritually. Translation gives us an entirely new sense of things, and gives us a new language. Old terms have a new meaning. This new meaning, or new sense of things, is called by Mrs. Eddy "religion's 'new tongue'."

When we translate into the new tongue, we change what we have been calling matter or material substance back into the original spiritual meaning. Mrs. Eddy says, "'The new tongue' is the spiritual meaning as opposed to the material. It is the language of Soul instead of the senses; it translates matter into its original language, which is Mind, and gives the spiritual instead of the material signification."

"Honest, Unselfish, and Pure"

As stated before, Mrs. Eddy admonishes us that our thought must not only become spiritualized in order to apprehend Spirit, but "it must become honest, unselfish, and pure, in order to have the least understanding of God in divine Science."

As I pondered this word *honesty*, it came to me that in order to have the least understanding of God in divine Science, we must be as honest in our thinking as divine Principle is honest. To be honest, our reliance on material things must be transferred to a perception of, and dependence upon, spiritual things. There is only one honesty. Therefore, any degree of honesty that we see or know humanly must identify divine Principle. A personal sense of honesty is always better than dishonesty, but honesty as a personal virtue is merely a sense of personal goodness and is devoid of the Principle of honesty.

It requires understanding on our part to discern between honesty as God's idea and a false sense of honesty, which is the lie of personality endeavoring to make itself equal with God. A personal sense of honesty seeks to glorify person, but in Christian Science our one motive for being honest is to glorify God. And we glorify God and manifest honesty as spiritual power, only as our thinking identifies divine Principle.

Next, in order to have an understanding of God in divine Science, we must be unselfish. What does it mean to be unselfish or unselfed? It does not mean a personal virtue. Unselfishness is spiritual selfhood. To be unselfish we think in terms of the one Mind, the one man, the one body. Unselfishness is the Christ-idea loved, understood, and lived. Unselfishness as a personal virtue includes minds many, personal wills, and personal desires. We often see human motherhood and fatherhood showing forth a very false sense of unselfishness. Since man identifies God, this fact excludes any selfhood apart from God. To see and know God as one and all, is to be unselfish or unselfed in our thinking. When we give up a personal sense of ourself and let God be all, then we manifest spiritual power.

Our thought must be pure in order to understand God. Pure thought is always associated with the one infinite Mind, and never with mind in a so-called material body. Pure thought does not originate with persons. Its source and origin are in God, and forever reflected forth as man's pure thinking and feeling and knowing.

As our thought becomes spiritualized so that it apprehends Spirit, as it becomes honest, unselfish, and pure, to the degree that it understands God in divine Science, there is a corresponding spiritual power manifested in our so-called human existence, our so-called human body, and our so-called material world.

Spiritual power is the result of the spiritualization of our thought. God's ideas require no spiritualizing process. They are already spiritual. It is only the human concepts that need to be improved and spiritualized through translation.

Mrs. Eddy has translated the spiritual originals into language that is comprehensible to us. Likewise, we should strive to translate the originals of all ideas and qualities that appear in our consciousness into thoughts and language that are comprehensible to us and to others.

All too often we repeat statements from our textbook with no attempt on our part to translate our thought of them back into Spirit, or the new tongue. It is only through translation that our human concepts are improved and our spiritual power is increased. It is only through translation that we have the signs following.

5. THE THEOLOGY OF JESUS

Mrs. Eddy is emphatically insistent that our thought must become spiritualized, that through translation our thought must become honest, unselfish and pure. And she is even more insistent that the students of Christian Science must understand the theology of Jesus in order to have the signs following that Jesus had because of his theology.

In *Pulpit and Press* we read: "The theology . . . of Christian Science [which is the theology that Jesus had] is contained in the volume entitled 'Science and Health with Key to the Scriptures.'" Mrs. Eddy says in *Science and Health*, "It was this theology of Jesus which healed the sick and sinning. It is his theology in this book and the spiritual meaning of this theology, which heals the sick and causes the sinning to 'forsake his way, and the unrighteous man his thoughts'."

The theology of Jesus was the scientific knowledge of Truth that he entertained in his consciousness. His theology was his own divine Mind, or his own divine intelligence. His theology was not a theory, but a demonstrable Science, called by Mrs. Eddy Christian Science or divine Science. The theology that Jesus used was capable of proof and was demonstrated by Jesus in healing the sick and the sinning, raising the dead, and walking over the waves.

There is a great difference between the theology of Jesus and the theologies of many different systems of religion. Religion is a term which covers an immense field ranging from the most primitive faith up to the highest spiritual understanding. But religion in its broadest sense is the affection and conduct expressed through the individual's highest human concept of God. The theology of all systems, except Christian Science, is based more or less on creeds and doctrines.

To a great extent, the theology of all systems of religion, except Christian Science, is scholastic theology. Much of what these religions know about God and man had been gained from the theological seminaries, and savors of human intellect and reason, based on a human concept of God and man. Scholastic theology is quite different in its nature from the divine theology that was taught and practiced by Jesus.

We must not forget that scholastic theology has done much for the human race. Any sincere belief in God does much for mankind. The scholastic theology of the Christian church has kept alive the Christ, and this alone has been a marvelous contribution to religious growth. But the scholastic theology as taught by Christian churches does not redeem the human race from matter, sin, sickness, and death.

There are more than two hundred Christian religions that are founded on creeds and doctrines, besides the many so-called heathen religions. The question is often asked, "Are all religions, in their last analysis, a question of creeds, doctrines, rites, and ceremonies?" It is true that the significance of true religion is often lost in the multitude of interpretations imposed upon it. The word *religion* is usually identified with minor moralities, conventional forms, technical orthodoxies, ecclesiasticisms, cultisms, and denominationalisms.

But true religion or vital Christianity is not based on creeds or doctrines, and it is not necessarily found in lofty cathedrals. Christian people believe that vital Christianity is essential in the saving of mankind, and that pure religion is the hope of salvation. There are thousands of persons desiring a practical religion, a living faith, a deeper understanding of God and man, and they will find it in the divine theology of Jesus as set forth in the Bible and the Christian Science textbook.

Pure religion, with all the divine ideas and qualities, is to be found only in the human heart. These ideas and qualities which constitute pure religion are utilized and expressed visibly in art, in science, in music, in literature, in statesmanship, in business, in pretty much anything else to which the individual may devote his thought.

Association Address of 1944

Truly religious individuals are not confined entirely to ritualistic forms and scholastic theories, any more than they were in our Lord's time. Truly religious individuals represent or evidence forth the Christ ideas and qualities, and are today recasting the whole human concept for a higher mode of life; the Christ-life within the individual is becoming visible universally as one holy church — as one spiritualized consciousness.

This is as it should be. The Christian churches, as a whole, were never more truly religious in their relations than they are today. Their one need is the control and guidance of the Christ, Truth, within, as revealed through Christian Science. And unless many signs are misleading, this inner light of understanding, this impersonal Christ within, is breaking forth anew in numerous modes and methods.

Each one of us needs to be redeemed, more and more, from scholastic theology. Each of us has much false scholastic theology clinging to us that we are practically unaware of, even though we classify ourselves as Christian Scientists. It is this scholastic theology that is hindering us from expressing to the world that inner light — that Christ within which permits of "signs following." We should examine ourselves and see to what extent our thought is the teaching of false theology.

For instance, do we believe that we were ever born? Do we believe that we have a personal life that lives in a personal body? Do we believe that we as a personality are sinners and must be saved from sin? Do we believe that we as a personality can become sick and die? Do we believe that we can be poor, wretched, and robbed, and dominated? Do we believe in evil, in war, in storms, in shipwrecks, in the lack of tax money? In other words, do we believe in another power and presence, other than the one Almighty God? Do we believe that we individually are other than this one Almighty God in expression? If so, we are accepting false theology as our religion.

Mrs. Eddy says, "Scholastic theology makes God manlike; Christian Science [or the theology of Jesus] makes man Godlike."

She also says, "Popular theology makes God tributary to man, coming at human call; whereas the reverse is true in Science." It is quite true that the theology of Jesus is today shaking creedal and doctrinal foundations which have been believed to be solid for time and eternity.

Our Concept of God and Man

Generally speaking, we might say that before Christian Science revealed the theology of Jesus, our concept of God was the unknown God, whom we ignorantly worshiped. Our concept of God was that He was wholly apart from us and governed us very much as a mother governs her child, rewarding us according to worthiness or unworthiness.

But now our concept of God is greatly enlarged. We understand God numerically as one Being, as one whole and all. We think of God as an infinite incorporeal Being, the only Being, the very being of each one of us. We think of God as the only consciousness, and we know there is no other consciousness. We do not think of consciousness as the effect of God or Mind, or as produced by God or Mind, but that God or Mind, in fact, is consciousness, and there is no other consciousness. We think of God or Mind or consciousness as all-inclusive, as an inseparable, indivisible unity of good. We think of God or Mind or consciousness as revealing Himself to Himself, since there is none outside of Himself or beside Himself to whom He can reveal Himself. We think of God as one infinite self. We think of God as His own interpreter.

Before Christian Science revealed the theology of Jesus to us, we believed that man was a personal, material, mortal existence, wholly apart from God. We believed that the mind and body of man could be separated. We believed that sin, sickness, and death were inescapable.

But now our concept of man is greatly enlarged. We have learned that the Science of being includes man. Think of the sum total of all that God or Mind brings into expression — that is man. Think of the full representation of what God or Mind is mentally and spiritually — that is man. Think of God or Mind presenting Himself infinitely, presenting His faculties, His all-seeing and all-knowing, His infinite operations and movements, all-energy, all- action, what these are consciously to Him, as Himself — that is man.

Think of God or Mind as presenting Himself, again and again, to Himself, never twice alike, presenting His spiritual senses, His infinite elements of form, color, quality and quantity — that is man. Think of God or Mind presenting again and again, His beauty, His art, His order, His immensity — that is man as reflection or evidence. Man represents or evidences, infinitely and consciously, all that God, his Mind, is.

Let us think of man as the infinite intelligence of God or Mind, as the omniscience, omnipresence and omnipotence of God. Let us think of man as the immanence of God or Mind, as the compound of infinite ideas indwelling in their cause or divine Principle. Let us think of man — the spiritual compound idea — as the subjectiveness or the essence of what God is, as Himself. What God or Mind knows Himself to be — man is that.

A ray of light is the sun's own shining. So let us think of each one of us right here as God's own shining. Let us think of each one of us right here as God's own conscious living, as God's own conscious loving, as God's own conscious understanding, as God's own conscious creating, as God's own conscious being. Man is the conscious activeness of God or Mind. All that God or Mind senses Himself to be is man in His image and likeness.

God or Mind is presenting Himself at this time, as man, in far greater usefulness, far greater activity, a far greater measure of abundance and sublimity than we have ever known before. Life is being expressed more and more in its original buoyancy, freshness, fairness, and freedom from restrictions.

Someone will say, all this that you say about man is beautiful, but it is far beyond what we can demonstrate in our present age. But let us not forget that God or Mind demonstrates His own allness. All things are possible to God. He is a living conscious power that demonstrates itself. He presents Himself in tangible, concrete proofs or demonstrations as man and the universe.

Our part as Christian Scientists is to abide in the spiritual fact that we are God's image and likeness, that we are spiritual, not material, that we are, not shall be, perfect and immortal. We should not let the accuser be a law unto us, but we should be a law unto ourselves.

God and Man as One Being

I should like to repeat two paragraphs that we used at the beginning of this lesson. Whenever we make the statements that "God and man is one inseparable being" or that "Principle and its idea is one," these statements may mean much to us in Christian Science, or they may be mere words to us. This oneness means that man alone can do nothing. It means that God alone, without man, can do nothing, cannot even exist. Whatever is done within the realm of the spiritual universe, God alone without man does not do it. Whatever is done, whatever the circumstance, or the event, God and man do it together as one inseparable being.

If there were such a thing as sin in the world, it would be God and man sinning as one inseparable sin. If there were such a thing as death in the world, it would be God and man as one inseparable being, dying and being death. Since we cannot attach sin and death to God, we cannot attach them to man, because God and man is one inseparable being. God without man cannot be immortal. God and man as one inseparable being is immortal, is Life eternal.

This understanding that God and man is one inseparable being is indeed our Saviour. This is the divine theology taught by Jesus and presented to the world as Christian Science by Mary Baker Eddy in *Science and Health with Key to the Scriptures*.

ABOUT THE AUTHOR: The papers of Martha Wilcox deal with the subjective consciousness and how it can be changed through an understanding of God. Mrs. Wilcox shows that change is inevitable when we treat the inner self through prayer as taught in Christian Science. The strong point of her writing is her emphasis on the need to so spiritualize the subjective self that it results in healing.

Martha Wilcox was a prominent teacher during the years when the Christian Science organization was at its peak of prosperity. She grew up on a farm in Kansas, under the influence of a religious family life. She studied privately for a Teacher's Certificate and became a teacher in the local schools. Before finding Christian Science, she was an active member of the Methodist Church. It was through a series of events, in which she sought medical aid for her ailing husband, that she was presented in 1902 with a copy of *Science and Health.* As she studied and pondered this book, she was healed of a physical problem of long-standing. While her husband was not interested in Christian Science, she definitely was.

Within the next six years, she had Primary class instruction, became an active member of a branch church in Kansas City, Missouri, and managed to devote much of her time to the healing work, in addition to caring for her family. In 1908 she received a call from The Mother Church in Boston asking her to serve Mrs. Eddy at her home in Chestnut Hill, Massachusetts.

In Mrs. Wilcox's first interview with Mrs. Eddy, it was impressed upon her that everything in one's experience is subjective or mental. Mrs. Wilcox writes of this interview: "[Mrs. Eddy], no doubt, realized that at my stage of growth, I thought of creation — that is, all things — as separated into two groups, one group spiritual and the other group material. But during this lesson I caught my first glimpse of the fact that all right, useful things — which I had been calling 'the unrighteous mammon' — were mental and represented spiritual ideas. She showed me that unless I were faithful and orderly with the objects of sense that made up my present mode of consciousness, there would never be revealed to me the 'true riches,' or the progressively higher revealments of substance and things."

Mrs. Wilcox later wrote: "I well remember when for the first time I understood that everything of which I am conscious is thought, and never external to or separate from what I call my mind, and that which I call my mind is not always seeing things as they actually are."

In 1910, Mrs. Wilcox was recommended by Mrs. Eddy for Normal Class instruction, with Bicknell Young as teacher. This was the beginning of a long and successful career for Mrs. Wilcox as a practitioner and teacher. In 1911, she taught her first class. Until her passing in 1948, she was dedicated to serving the Christian Science movement, and became one of the most respected teachers in the Field. She was the author of many profound papers on Christian Science, mainly papers given each year to her association of students.

Mrs. Wilcox's two years with Mrs. Eddy equipped her to understand so well the subjective nature of all things. She explains how to shift the focal point of thought from the objective world of people, things, happenings, to the subjective world of intuitions, thoughts, ideas. Although she stresses the mental cause of disease and discord, she goes beyond an analysis of the human mind and explains how to relate to God subjectively through prayer; how to develop an understanding of Him that spiritualizes consciousness and heals, how to transcend the false material view of creation and find the spiritual view.

At the time that Mrs. Wilcox wrote these addresses, the Church organization would not permit the publication or circulation of such papers. But Mrs. Wilcox did share them privately with students, and they were handed down over the years to the present time. In giving these papers to her students, it is possible that Mrs. Wilcox hoped they would someday go forth to bless the world, for surely she must have been aware of their timeless message.

For further information regarding Christian Science:
Write: The Bookmark
         Post Office Box 801143
         Santa Clarita, CA 91380
Call: 1-800-220-7767
Visit our website: www. thebookmark.com